Charlie Brandt, Serial Killer : An Anthology of True Crime

Pete Dove

Published by Trellis Publishing, 2021.

While every precaution has been taken in the preparation of this book, the publisher assumes no responsibility for errors or omissions, or for damages resulting from the use of the information contained herein.

CHARLIE BRANDT, SERIAL KILLER : AN ANTHOLOGY OF TRUE CRIME

First edition. June 28, 2021.

Copyright © 2021 Pete Dove.

ISBN: 979-8224373215

Written by Pete Dove.

CHARLIE BRANDT, SERIAL KILLER

PETE DOVE

Keeping it in the Family

'Michelle was extremely loyal,' said her close friend, Debbie Knight, 'she was giving, she was caring, she was dedicated. An amazing woman.'

Lisa Emmons concurred. 'Michelle was fun so smart and organized,'

It had been a long time since her many friends had seen the successful executive, or even heard from her. In Michelle's case, a long time being more than a couple of days. That was unusual, in fact so strange that these friends began to worry. In the end, tensions rose, and Debbie decided that she had to visit. The increasingly alarmed messages that she had left on Michelle's answer phone had not been answered, and the probability that something bad had happened to her friend could be ignored no longer. Even so, none of these concerned women could have had the slightest idea of the extremes of violence they would discover.

Michelle was born in 1966. She was a single woman, a career driven successful executive with Orlando's Golf Channel. When her body was discovered, in 2004, she was just thirty-seven years old. Events had begun to come together towards their tragic ending on Friday September 2nd, 2004. Thanks to the growing threat of a hurricane out in the Atlantic, the Florida Keys had been evacuated. That was a cause of concern to Michelle, living further north in the state, because her aunt and uncle resided in this risky region. However, she invited them up to the relative safety of her home and was delighted when they agreed to come. By the following Wednesday, Michelle's mother was getting worried. She had phoned each evening to check on how things were going, to speak with her niece and her sister, Teri. All that she could get was a voicemail message.

Michelle's mother, Mary Lou, had contacted Debbie, worried about her own difficulties in getting in touch with her daughter. She asked her to go check on the three people she believed were staying at the property.

As Debbie arrived at the tidy, white fronted house, shaded now in the dark of the evening, she noticed that the only light that was on was in the garage. She got out of her car, and moved towards the front door, only to see the mail poking out of the box. A peer through the window showed an untidy pile of letters and small packages gathered on the floor. Debbie's concerns became stronger still. Something was wrong. That sense of unrest was heightened by the fact that Michelle's Uncle Charlie's car stood in the drive, but there was no evidence of any life in the home. A two-day old newspaper lay wrapped on the lawn. While the presence of Charlie's car was reassuring, meaning that he and his wife were still there, nothing else about the scene promoted calm.

Debbie was a close enough friend of Michelle to hold a key to her home. She decided that it was time to go inside. The key though, would not work. It seemed as though the latch had been dropped on the inside, or some other obstruction was stopping the door from opening. Next, she decided to head towards the faint glow coming from the garage. The door to this was accessed around the side of the property, and as she made her way there, the glow brightened through the glass paned door. She approached, looked through and saw Charlie Brandt dangling, dead, his body hanging from a beam in the garage, a bedsheet tied around his throat.

Rob Hemmert was with the Seminole County Sherriff's office and became lead investigator in the case. He was sent out to the scene and attended along with other officers who had arrived following a panicked call from Lisa. She recalls them breaking into the home, being inside for under a minute, then rushing out. One threw up there and then on the lawn. Whatever was inside that innocent seeming house was bad.

'I'd worked hundreds of similar investigations,' recalled Hemmert, 'but I'd not seen anything like this before, and I probably never will again.'

Inside her bedroom Michelle Jones' body lay on her bed, at rest. It was not her complete body, however. Her head had been removed and sat, tidily placed, next to her.

In the lounge, Teri was positioned on the couch. She had at least seven stab wounds in her body. One, maybe more, had proved fatal. Closer inspection revealed that Michelle's body had not just been decapitated, but her heart had been gouged out of her body.

'I could not believe what I was seeing,' said Hemmert. There was no evidence of a struggle, a fight or even an argument. Hemmert quickly came to an inevitable conclusion. Brandt had murdered his wife and niece, killing them sadistically and with uncontrolled violence, then hung himself. Nobody else appeared to be involved in this crime. First impressions are often correct as, indeed, they were in this case.

It was left to Debbie to break the news to Michelle's parents. 'I told her dad; it was the worst thing ever. My best friend's father, and I was just screaming,' revealed Debbie.

It seems as though on the night she died; Michelle had arranged for Lisa to come over. Charlie and Teri had been due to leave, the hurricane having passed. However, some kind of dispute had arisen between the married couple. Charlie had insisted on staying, even though Hemmert found their bags packed and waiting in the hall.

Michelle phoned Lisa earlier on that evening cancelling the dinner date, because her Aunt and uncle were arguing and not good company. It was the last time Lisa heard from her friend. Evidence in the kitchen suggested that a meal had been cooked, fish of some sort, and the three had settled down to drink wine. That was September 13th, 2004. Two days later their bodies were found.

'It was just inconceivable that he could have killed them,' said Mary Lou. She had known Charlie for seventeen years, and he had always come across as mild mannered. A gentle soul who would not harm anybody, or anything except perhaps the fish he lifted from the ocean. She could not have known that deep within her brother in law lay a volcano threatening to erupt, one that did so with frightening regularity, it was later theorized. When dormant, it was ruggedly peaceful, and idyllic. When the pressure burst, the results were terrifying.

Lisa and Debbie saw a slightly different side to Charlie, but still not one that raised any alarm bells. 'We used to call him "eccentric",' explained Lisa. The found the way he referred to his niece always by the name 'Victoria Secret' odd, although not worryingly so. He seemed an ideal match to Teri, who was easy going, carefree in fact. Her laissez faire approach to life seemed perfect to give Charlie the freedom to bounce around in his own more changeable world.

Teri's closest friend was Melanie Fetcher: 'She was the best friend you could ever have. If my husband could love me one third as much as Charlie loved Teri, I would be the happiest woman in the whole world,' she said, describing the seemingly deeply loving relationship her best friend and her husband shared. 'They never argued, I never saw him get angry,' she continued.

Indeed, their relationship seemed to almost border on the twee. For example, they would prepare lunch for each other, because, as Rob Hemmert explained, 'Lunch tasted better when it was prepared by one who loves you.' With such a loving relationship, it seemed impossible that Charlie could grab one of his niece's kitchen knives and stab the woman he adored with it no less than seven times.

But then a truth of equally disturbing proportions began to emerge. Charlie Brandt's older sister, Angela, asked to speak to the officer leading the investigation. When she met with Hemmert, he could not believe what she had to tell him.

Brandt's relatives had been called together for a briefing led by police. Angela, though, did not show up. She was waiting in the parking lot, clearly distressed. Later, she told officers that she had important information to impart.

In order to gain a better insight into Charlie Brandt's personality – note, we could never claim to understand what was happening inside the killer's head – we must travel back in time to another occasion when he lost control. January 3rd, 1971. Charlie is barely into his teens, just thirteen years old. Older sister Angela is fifteen.

It is a normal evening for this normal family that is, in a few moments of indescribable violence, about to be permanently changed. Angela is, like most teens like to be, in her room. Her dad is shaving and her mom running a bath.

The first indication that anything might be wrong wrong is a strangled scream from the father: 'Charlie, don't!' he voices. It is too late. His son is carrying a gun. Charlie fires into his father's back, and seeing the man collapse in front of him turns his attention to his mother, horrified and helpless in the bath. He fires again and again into her body. Ilse is eight months pregnant. 'Angela, call the police,' gasps the fatally injured woman. Charlie turns the gun towards his sister now and pulls the trigger.

By chance the weapon seizes. Charlie lunges at his sister, and she sees that the child in front of her is not the brother she knew. 'I saw the madness, the glazed over look,' she said later. The two wrestle, Angela desperately trying to calm her younger brother down. She tells him over and over again that she loves him.

Suddenly, he changes. She recalled seeing the glazed expression leave him and the usual Charlie reinhabit his features. 'You're not going to leave me, are you?' the small child pleaded. In the police interview she gave back in 2004, she describes (through a breaking voice) how she fled through the door, screaming. How she ran barefoot and in a torn and bloodied night dress through the freezing Indiana snow to the home of a neighbor. How she pounded on their front door. Sandy Radcliffe was those neighbors' sixteen-year-old daughter, and she remembered the panic in the ringing of the doorbell, the crashes on their front door. Then the tone changed, to a calmer, quieter knocking.

Sandy reached the door, and opened it to see a small, frightened boy standing there. Angela had rushed on to the home of another neighbor. Her brother had taken her place at the Radcliffe's door.

'Sandy', said the figure in front of her, 'I just shot my mom and dad.'

'He had the blackest eyes of anybody I ever say,' remembered Sandy.

Herbert survived, but Ilse, and her unborn baby, died. What makes this story even more tragic, and even more surprising is that it could not have been predicted. The Brandt family were a close knit, loving unit.

Charlie, proper name Carl but always known by as Charlie, was the second of four children born to Herbert and Ilse. They were German immigrants who had settled in the States some years before, originally in Texas. They had moved to Connecticut, and frequently changed locations as Herbert rose through the ranks of the International Harvester company. Starting as a laborer, he achieved promotions as a draftsman and eventually became a well-paid project engineer. Charlie had been born in 1957, and the family's frequent moves did not sit comfortably with him; he always required time to adjust to his new surroundings. Aged eleven they moved to Fort Wayne in Indiana.

One constant though was that the family liked to holiday in Florida. It was there that Charlie came close to his father, learning to fish and hunt. Back in Fort Wayne, Indiana, the family occupied a neat, white painted house. Not too big and not too small. In fact, an ordinary, comfortable home. For an ordinary, comfortable family.

Charlie adored his parents, and especially his mother. The two were intensely close. 'He was a mother's boy,' recalled Sandy Radcliffe with clarity borne from a mind that frequently wandered back to the events of 1971. Given this closeness, what could have triggered such inexplicable and extreme violence? Something he perpetrated once more, some third of a century later. And, possibly, at other times during his otherwise normal life.

Who knows, could the 'eccentricity' Debbie Knight saw in her best friend's uncle have been evidence of whatever demons lived inside his head? Or, would killing one's mother, and attempting to murder your father, inevitable turn somebody away from a state of consistent normality?

Dan Fiegal was in charge of the investigation back in 1971. On receiving the call, he sped to the Fort Wayne Hospital, hoping to find Herbert Brandt alive. He knew that Ilse was already dead. 'I don't know why my son did this, I have no ideas as to why my son did this,'; Herbert was alive, but he could offer no reason for this sudden, unexpected murderous behavior.

Fiegal took the child into custody, but the boy was in shock. He too had no idea why he had acted as he had. Back in 1971 understanding of the human mind was minimal in the extreme. It is little better understood today, although we do know that chemical changes present during puberty can lead to changes in the function of the brain. However, this does not explain why a boy would murder a mother he adored and attempt to kill a father and sister he loved.

He was sent for three separate psychological tests. One of these was with a psychiatrist, Ronald Pancner. His findings differed little from those of the doctors conducting the other tests. Their conclusions were, unhelpfully, that Charlie's actions were not explainable through the limited understanding of psychiatry held in those early 1970s' days.

'I was looking for mental illness,' explained Pascner, whose report listed many conditions from which the boy was not suffering, but none that were inflicting him. 'He was not showing any signs of serious mental illness. That was what I thought the court wanted to know. He did well at school, he did not get into any trouble, he loved his family,' continued the still bemused doctor many years later, after Charlie had killed once more. 'We thought he was a loving kid. There wasn't anything to diagnose.'

At thirteen years of age, under Indiana law, Charlie Brandt was considered too young to be held criminally guilty of his crimes. As a result, he was never charged with the murder of his mother, nor was he ever brought to trial for any of the actions he had committed. Instead, his case was investigated by a grand jury, and their conclusion was that he needed psychiatric treatment. It is very hard to believe from today's perspective that Charlie Brandt was not suffering from any psychological illness, but back then, the best in the business could find nothing amiss that might explain his behavior. It is hard to treat an illness you cannot identify. The Grand Jury's conclusion – 'Such anti-social conduct might repeat itself in the future' – might have been portentous, but it was hardly helpful to a team of doctors charged with treating a boy who appeared to be in a state of perfectly fine mental health.

Charlie spent just over a year housed in a psychiatric institute, a foreboding building that spoke of straight jackets and heavily medicated inmates. We do not have a clear picture of what happened to Charlie during that year, but it is hard to imagine that it was anything but hell for a boy who had done wrong, a very bad wrong, but had no idea why he had done it. Guilt must surely have weighed down his every waking second.

But on the outside, Herbert was recovering, and once he was as well as could be expected, he had another goal to achieve. Securing the release of his son and bringing him back into the family. If Herbert had ever cast blame upon the son he knew and loved (as opposed to the one who emerged for just a few moments on that fateful day), it was forgiven. However, he could not remain with the boy in Indiana. The story had made the news, inevitably, despite the boy's tender years, and few people were as understanding as Herbert.

Once Charlie was released back into his care, he took the entire family across the country to Florida, there to start a new life. A year later, Herbert married again, and moved on. For an unidentified reason

Charlie did not go with them. By now fifteen, he went into the care of his grandparents. Was the fear that he might attack his new stepmom too great? Was he resentful of the new woman in the family's life? Did something happen which scared the new woman of the household? Whatever the reason for the breakup of the family once more, it was not discussed. Like the other defining point of the family's existence. That January evening in 1971 was not to be mentioned again. It would be a secret borne by just three people, Herbert, Angela and Charlie himself. Even his two younger sisters, too young to understand what had happened to their mother, were denied the truth.

Whether this decision was right or not is down to our personal perspective. At one extreme, some people will claim that at least two more human beings, three if we include Charlie himself, could still be alive had the boy been incarcerated for life. On the other, there will be those who argue, persuasively and with moral right on their side, that the actions were those of a boy who did not know why he had fired that gun. And neither did the finest psychiatrists of the time. The actions were inexplicable, and under those circumstances a young child should not bear lifelong punishment for what he had done.

Hindsight is a wonderful thing. But even with this, we should not judge the way Herbert reacted. The man had lost his wife, unexpectedly and in perhaps the most terrible circumstances it is possible to perceive. It is understandable that he would not be prepared to lose his only son as well.

Yet, quite understandably, Mary Lou Jones cannot accept this. 'There is something wrong with a system that allows a thirteen-year-old boy to kill his mother, to try to kill his father and older sister, and nothing was done.' Her opinion is, under the terrible circumstances she faces herself, totally reasonable. Her ongoing anger is something with which it easy to empathize. Even when it is directed against a husband who lost his wife at the hands of his son 'He has never made a single effort to say how sorry he is that this has happened to us,' she said of Herbert.

Debby Knight, too, shows severe anger towards the father for his failure to tell people of the crime his son had committed. 'Charlie's father should be exposed; he knew what his son did. I'd love to find him sitting right next to me, because I'd find him guilty.' Debbie Knight's continuing bitterness is again easy to understand but does overlook the fact that many thirteen-year olds do strange and disturbing things; often it is not possible to identify why they commit these wrong doings. That does not mean that they should be tainted for life. The power of hindsight can distort what is right.

As for Charlie, life continued. He earned his degree in electronics in 1984 and a couple of years later was introduced, by way of his brother in law, to the woman who would become his wife. By this time, that brother in law was separated from Charlie's sister, Angela, and although he knew of the family history, he too believed that whatever issue had possessed the boy, the adult had outgrown. None of the Brandt family was invited to the wedding. Despite the story of an immensely close and supportive set up, it maybe was not as united as the public front appeared. Then again, when a son murders his mother, shoots his father and attacks his sister, there are bound to be aftershocks which last for many years. Charlie moved with Teri to a comfortable house in Big Pine Key in the Florida Keys. He worked as an engineer, a radar technician, and for many years, it seemed, life continued quietly and calmly.

The investigation into the deaths of Teri Brandt and Michelle Jones took investigator Rob Hemmert four hundred miles south to the Brandt's pleasant home. What he found raised an eyebrow on the experienced detective's features. Charlie had prepared for the coming hurricane. Obsessively. Every window was covered with a perfectly cut piece of wood, every door protected in a similar way. He had even cut perfectly sized slots through which the door handles could protrude. He was not an engineer for nothing!

The home was as immaculate inside as the perfectly cut protective panels might suggest. But Hemmert made an unusual discovery in the Brandt's bedroom. Behind the door hung a large, full length poster. Of a human female, the muscles and bones exposed. The sort of poster that might hang in a High School science lab, or in the office of a doctor or professor. Not the sort of wall art that most people would enjoy.

The Brandts' – one or both – fascination with human anatomy became more apparent as the search of their home continued. More posters, books and manuals came to light. Whilst this fascination was not hidden away, it is still an unusual hobby, (and struck Rob Hemmert as such) for a couple of members of the public to enjoy. Neither held any medical qualifications, they were not first aiders, and they were not (as far as anybody knew) planning to embark on a career in the field of medicine. If the collection belonged to just one of them, then the other partner must surely have felt a sense of unease. For Hemmert, it was clear that it was Charlie who was the one with the interest. He felt the view was confirmed when inside one anatomy book he discovered a newspaper cutting of a human heart. Clearly, it seemed, what had been done to Michelle was an echo of the findings in that immaculately tidy house.

There was more. Victoria's Secret is a retailer specializing in lingerie, especially for younger people. Charlie liked to collect their brochures. Several copies were discovered, addressed to him. It seems as though the pet name he held for his niece was perhaps not as innocent as it might appear. Indeed, Hemmert suspects it was always his intention to kill his niece. Perhaps not on that September evening, because surely, he would not have left behind such incriminating evidence of his infatuation, if that is what he held, behind. But, according to Hemmert, killing and dismembering her was always his goal.

Brandt's internet use was even more alarming than his collection of twenty somethings' lingerie magazines. His penchant was for hard core pornography of the most extreme kind, his search for 'necrobabes' indicating one of the perverted interests he held. Indeed, it seemed any site that portrayed sexual violence towards women attracted his attention. 'Hypnobabes', 'Gothic Death Killer', the list was long and unpleasant.

Hemmert developed a further, frightening hypothesis. Charlie Brandt's dismembering of his niece was extremely neatly done. If police had not known better, it would have been easy to assume the ghastly work belonged to a surgeon or coroner, so accurately were the cuts into her body made. In order to gain such competence, assumed Hemmert, he would have needed to have carried out other attacks.

A large-scale search of cold cases was undertaken. Possible connections flooded in, but they were tenuous. Police forces were keen to be able to solve long held mysteries, yet if Charlie Brandt was responsible for any, then he had covered his tracks well. In the end, twenty-six potential homicides were linked to him. Among these were twelve-year-old Carol Sullivan, who disappeared from a school bus stop in 1978; Darlene Toler disappeared from Miami and Lisa Saunders was dragged from her car much closer to home, in Big Pine Key. Each of these victims were mutilated, with their hearts or heads removed. The strongest link to Charlie Brandt was Sherry Perisho, a homeless woman who lived on a dinghy in Big Pine Key. Her body was discovered less than a thousand feet from Brandt's home, and he also matched a sketch made from a witness statement. However, because his back story was not known, Charlie did not fall under suspicion at the time.

But although the possibility must exist that Brandt killed more than just the three members of his family, proof of such was not possible to find. Could he have appeared as such a quiet and kindly person while hiding a violent truth? Did Teri have suspicions? She told a relative once of fears that Charlie had done something wrong when he appeared at home late at night covered in blood. He excused that by saying he had been gutting fish, but the explanation seemed unlikely,

Her diaries also demonstrated that he sometimes stayed out all night. But not coming home when expected, gutting fish at night, collecting lingerie catalogs and even watching hard porn might be disturbingly unusual, and certainly would cause discomfort amongst friends and family, yet they are not the evidence of a man who killed regularly.

It would be interesting if Charlie could be seen by a psychiatrist today. Perhaps a reason behind his extraordinary behavior might suggest itself. Perhaps some evidence of a man suffering from multiple personalities could emerge. Maybe something in his childhood had happened for which, deep down, he blamed his parents, and especially his mother. After all, mothers are there to protect, and if they fail to do this, albeit through no fault of their own, psychologists know that extreme reactions can be invoked. But extreme enough for Charlie to kill Ilse? Surely not. Perhaps his anger was linked to her pregnancy, did he suffer from a form of autism which meant he could not cope with the major change about to impact on his life? Was this fear and anger magnified by the fact that Charlie was entering early adolescence?

Yet such ideas can never be more than conjecture. The chance of finding the truth disappeared when Charlie decided that enough was enough and chose to hang himself from the joists of his niece's garage.

BARBARA STAGER AND THE BLACK WIDOWS

SARAH REESON

Barbara Stager: A Black Widow

There are many stories of black widows, women who kill their husbands for power or financial gain. These women have been scattered throughout history and the ones who have been caught for their crimes often make us take a second to consider what the people we love, and believe love us, are truly capable of. You may never know whom you are sleeping next to, but should you really be concerned that they will poison your oatmeal or shoot you while you sleep? It's a rare occurrence, but it does happen.

One such case comes from the sleepy city of Durham, North Carolina. Durham was a tight knit town, a wholesome community where people were proud to raise their children, work, and attend their churches. And even decades later, the residences of Durham have not forgotten what happened when evil walked through their town.

In The Beginning

Barbara Ford, born Barbara Terry in 1948, is an average American woman to everyone who meets her. She has been happily married for almost ten years. She is a devout Christian and member of the community. She is a mother of two sons, Brian and Jason, both of which she loves deeply and she is an attentive wife.

No one questioned her story when her husband Larry Ford died, tragically according to Barbara, in an accidental shooting. While cleaning his firearm, a 25-caliber pistol, Larry accidentally shot himself in the chest and died from the injury. The police ruled this a suicide at first and then later changed their decision to an accidental shooting.

The whole town of High Point, North Carolina, where Barbara and Larry had called home with their two children, agreed that this was tragic but that there was nothing suspicious about it. The only ones to question what had happened to Larry were his family. They seemed to believe that there was no way Larry would "accidentally" shoot himself. Their suspicion fell on deaf ears, at the time, and they were left to wonder what had actually happened.

Meanwhile, Barbara Ford packed up her belongings and her two sons and moved back home to Durham, North Carolina, her hometown, to stay with her parents. To all appearances she was seeking solace from the loss of her first husband with family and attempting to rebuild a life for herself and her sons.

It took her very little time to find this new life.

Barbara settled into a new house in Durham with her two sons, a house that was just down the road from Russell Stager. Russell, or Russ to anyone who knew him, was currently going through a divorce from his first wife, Jo Lynn Snow, whom he had been married to for just under four years. High school sweethearts at the time, they found that life was taking them in different directions and despite the divorce they remained good friends.

Russ and Barbara hit things off rather immediately. The chemistry between the two was rather evident even if friends of Russ could not see why he was particularly drawn to her. Barbara inserted herself rather fully into his life and rather quickly after meeting him. They were inseparable. She attended the sporting events that he coached and participated in. She was openly affectionate with him. It was not difficult to see where things were going with the couple.

They were engaged in a few short months and before the ink had even dried on his divorce papers they were married.

A Happy Couple

Russ Stager was an upstanding member of the community. He was a high school gym teacher, he coached baseball, and he was a driver's education instruction. On the weekends he worked for the National Guard as a firearms instructor. And on Sundays he taught Sunday school with Barbara at the Baptist Church that they both were devoted members to.

Barbara Stager's life revolved around the church. She was involved, heavily, in a great deal of church activities. Whether it was youth activities, senior's events, or other charitable affairs, Barbara was often the first to volunteer to assist.

They appeared to be the perfect image of a happy couple. No one could say that they didn't appear to be happy together.

In the early years of their marriage they both spent extravagantly, catching the attention of their friends and co-workers. They had a beach house and a large family home. They were frequently purchasing new clothes and new cars. One friend joked, "When their car needed an oil change they just got a new car". That was the frequency that they purchased vehicles. They also became members of a very prestigious, local country club to add to their symbol of wealth.

Russ's co-workers were baffled by how he could afford this lifestyle on a teacher's salary and speculation began to spread about the type of payout Barbara must have received from the death of her first husband. The belief was that it must have been fairly substantial in order for them to spend and live the way they did.

They were a perfect couple. They were dedicated to each other. They were happy in their public life together. They were devout and dedicated Christians. They were the product of envy for many. It was all a little too good to be true.

Barbara got pregnant quickly into the marriage much to Russ's pleasure and surprise, but unfortunately she miscarried the child. This weighed heavily on Russ, who wanted children very badly. However, he later adopted Barbara's two sons as his own and spent his spare time raising them as he would his own sons. Russ felt that they needed a father figure in their life and that since they had lost their father at such a young age it was his job to fill that void. They were a complete family in image and legality at that point.

Barbara soon began a job at the local radio station as an advertisement sales person and she also revealed to Russ and their friends that she was working on a novel. This novel, titled 'Untimely Death', was about the death of her husband. She claimed that she had heard back from a major publishing company that wanted to pick up her novel and had offered her a sizable cash advance.

This was the cause for major celebration in the Stager household and among their friends and family. Barbara received nothing but support in her new venture from Russ and her friends at the country club were eager to see the release of this book.

This was also the beginning of what would be an avalanche of marital problems for Russ and Barbara. Things would began to crumble soon after these happy announcements and the once perfect, happy couple will face strain and hardship like they had never believed they would in the years to come.

Suspicion and Lies

It was in the year of 1982, only a couple years into Russ and Barbara's marriage, when the truth of their situation began to become very clear. And their situation was not nearly as comfortable as Russ had been lead to believe.

Russ, while at home one afternoon, discovered a box of unpaid bills that was hidden in the house. The amount of unpaid items was staggering. The amount of debt that they were in, the amount that he was unaware of, was shocking. When he confronted Barbara about it she insisted that she would take care of it, that she was handling it, but he was reluctant to believe her.

Immediately Russ took control over the household finances, as he no longer trusted Barbara to handle it as she had before. It was clear that she hadn't been handling it at all and they desperately needed to dig themselves out of this debt. They sold their beach house. They downsized their main house, twice, in order to dig themselves out of debt, and eventually Russ had to go to his parents for financial aid.

In the mean time, Barbara approached the bank with her cash advance letter from the publishing house and on that basis alone was allowed to received a $30 000 bank loan, a loan that she has no intention of paying back.

Despite the huge level of deceit associated with the unpaid bills and the debt, Russ stayed with Barbara. He forgave her for this incident and they tried to make their marriage work again for the sake of the two boys, for the sake of their family, a family that has so recently become whole.

However, as time passed people begin to get suspicious because Barbara's book was still not released. When she was questioned about it she would be evasive and she would push off the question. Her boss at the radio station called the publishing company to inquire about the upcoming book only to find out that they had no contract with Barbara Stager or for the title in question. He immediately went to Russ and informed him of this as well as the fact that Barbara hadn't been to work at the radio station in months.

Barbara's lies were beginning to pile up and it wasn't looking good for her. However, Russ did not approach her about them. He still wanted to preserve their marriage, their family. Family mattered to him above everything else.

In 1984 the next blow to their marriage was struck when Russ discovered that Barbara was having an affair. Russ saw her, in her car, in the middle of a passionate make-out session with another man. This affair tore a major hole in their marriage despite Russ's attempts to forgive her for it.

Barbara blamed Russ for the affair. She claimed that he didn't pay enough attention to her, and that he was never around. She was also aware that he'd had an affair on his first wife and she was potentially using the guilt of that as leverage to get herself out of her own actions. It is difficult to say for certain her motivations behind this particular deceit.

Regardless of the motivation or the fault, Russ forgave her as much as he could, like he had with all things in their marriage thus far and they continued to have a life together.

But Russ was not without his suspicion in the years to come. These are suspicions he confided in his ex-wife Jo Lynn Snow whom he would meet with regularly to discuss his life and problems. He quite often talked about how he felt betrayed by the affair. He also knew that Barbara was removing large sums of money from his accounts. And he felt paranoid about his safety with Barbara the more he learned about her first marriage and the questionable circumstances of her first husband's death.

His suspicions would prove to be more than simple paranoia and his confessions to Jo Lynn would be fundamental in assuring that an alternative narrative was considered in the investigation.

Things aren't always the way they seem at first and you can't always trust the words of a grieving widow.

A Fatal Morning

It was 6:08am on February 1, 1988 when the first responders were called the Stager household. Police and EMS arrived, filled with dread at being called to the home of a friend and esteemed member of the community.

When the EMS found Russ Stager in the bedroom with a gunshot wound to the back of his head he was still breathing, barely, and had a pulse. He was rushed to the hospital to seek further medical attention where he soon died of his injuries at the age of 44.

Upon their arrival at the home Barbara Stager was distraught. She kept saying to anyone who would listen that she had warned him about "those damn guns". And she was repeating this fact over and over again. The police had to remove her from the bedroom for the EMS workers to be able to work properly.

When questioned by the police, Barbara said that she'd been trying to remove the 25-caliber pistol that Russ kept under his pillow and it had discharged. She claimed it had a hair-trigger and it had gone off before she even realized it. Barbara said that he had begun to keep the 25-caliber pistol under his pillow recently for fear of prowlers and burglars that had recently been prominent in the neighbourhood.

Barbara insisted that she hated firearms, feared them even, and that she never wanted them anywhere near the bed. She had warned him about the gun and about having guns. She was always worried that he might mistake one of the kids as a burglar and shoot them.

The incident was ruled an accidental shooting almost immediately. There was no reason to suspect foul play.

When Captain Ricky Buchanan interviewed Barbara Stager the day after the shooting he encountered Barbara's father who had already taking the sheets from the bed to be laundered. Since the shooting had been ruled accidental, there was no restriction on cleaning up the scene. Captain Buchanan found the rest of the house tidy and the bedroom to look as though nothing had even occurred there. It was unsettling, but he could not put his finger on just why it didn't sit right with him.

His impression of Barbara was not what he would have expected for a grieving widow. She was a little distraught, but she was calmer than he believed someone who had just lost her husband tragically should be. Still, she stuck to her original story about the events of the previous evening. And when Captain Buchanan left the Stager house he couldn't help but feel there was something a little off about the entire situation. He couldn't put his finger on it, but there was something that was not quite right.

It was Jo Lynn Snow that would lead the police in the correct direction for this case. When she received word that Russ Stager had died in an 'accidental' shooting she knew that there was no truth in that. Russ had been obsessive about gun safety and she knew that he would never store a firearm loaded, let alone store it with the safety off, cocked, and with a round in the chamber. And there was no way he would keep a firearm underneath a pillow. It just wouldn't have happened.

Coupled with everything that Russ had confided in her in the last few years, Jo Lynn set out to compose a letter to the police department outlining everything she knew about Russ and Barbara's marriage and Russ's suspicions.

The word of a paranoid ex-wife was not enough to sway the investigating officer, until Jo Lynn pointed out that Barbara's first husband, ten years earlier, had also died of an accidental shooting. It was at this point that interests were peaked and suspicions were raised.

Some things in life were coincidence, but when it comes to murder there are very few coincidences.

The Unraveling Story

The investigation into Russ Stager's death continued, the initial belief of it being an accidental shooting suspended until further investigation can be done. Barbara maintained her original story. She reached under the pillow, withdrew the firearm, and it accidentally discharged.

Accidental shootings are common when firearms are improperly stored or kept in unsafe places. Barbara's story is plausible. However, when it is looked at under a microscope every aspect of it begins to fall apart.

Firearms expert Eugene Bishop investigated Barbara's claim that the gun had a hair-trigger. He examined the 25-caliber Beretta pistol and subjected it to a trigger test where weight is added to the trigger in one-pound increments until the weapon fires. It was determined that the firearm had a four-pound draw weight. This indicated that it would have required deliberate force to fire the pistol and that it would not have discharged if Barbara had just 'accidentally' touched the trigger as she claimed. This was the first hole in her story.

Additionally, Eugene Bishop test fired the weapon to determine where the spent casing would land. It was determined that the casing would land to the right and rear of the shooter. Looking at the photos from the crime scene, this did not match the position of the casing, which should have been near the middle of the bedspread to match Barbara's account, but was, instead, near the pillows. This indicated that the gun was either fired from a different position than Barbara claimed or that the bullet casing was moved after the weapon was fired. This was the second hole her story.

This discrepancy was further supported by a report from medical investigators that came out following the autopsy on Russ Stager's body. The bullet wound in the back of Russ's head did not match the situation that Barbara had described. The bullet's trajectory was wrong. The angle of the trajectory indicated that the shooter would have had to been above and behind Russ when firing the weapon, therefore firing it at a downward angle. For the trajectory to match Barbara's story of firing it from the bed, the trajectory would have been up from bed level and to the back of his head. This was not so. This was the third hole in her story.

To further confirm the trajectory of the bullet they re-examined the bed sheets that were on the bed when Russ Stager was shot. If the weapon had been fired from where Barbara indicated it had been then there would be gun shot residue on the bed sheets. This could be detected despite the fact that the sheets had been laundered. Despite being tested thoroughly, the investigators could find no gun shot residue on the sheets to indicate that the firearm had been discharged from the position that Barbara had indicated. This supported the theory that the weapon had indeed been fired from above and away from the bed. This further eroded the story that she had told.

In order to test out this ongoing theory Captain Buchanan had Barbara reenact the events of that evening in front of a video camera. Captain Buchanan went as far as to say, "I'm standing face to face with a killer. I know it, but she don't know I know it." He additionally added after the filming was complete, "there's no doubt at all that she intentionally shot and killed Russ Stager, no doubt."

When reviewing the videotape it became clear almost instantly that there were inconsistencies in her narrative. She kept trying to reposition the body and readjust herself to make the facts fit. And the story she was telling began to change and become less certain for the first time since it had all started.

The chips were pilling up against Barbara Stager, but there was still some digging left to be done. They needed to find a motivation. There needed to be more evidence. So they followed the money.

Barbara had a history of hiding debt and money from Russ, but the extent that was uncovered was shocking. Barbara had taken out a second loan to cover the coast of her first loan and she had brought the documentation home in order to obtain her husband's signature. Russ's will had recently been revised and there was a life insurance policy that had been taken out on Russ, also recently. In addition, several checks had been made out from Russ's account to Barbara's account for large sums of money. The suspicion around this was growing.

The police had Durward Matheny, a forensic documents examiner, review the second bank loan, the will, and the checks that had been put through just months before Russ Stager's death. He concluded that the second bank loan held a forged signature, the revised will held a forged signature, and the checks had also been forged. In addition, the life insurance policy, for which Barbara was the sole beneficiary for $200 000, all of his assets, and their $120 000 home, was also a forged document.

The evidence was staggering, but there was one last item to be discovered. In a locker at the high school Russ Stager worked at was a cassette tape that held his final words, recorded January 29, 1988 at 1:50pm. On the cassette Russ voiced his concerns about Barbara. He talked about how she would wake him up to give him what she indicated was Aspirin and then would stand there until he took it. He would never take it. "Why, if I was asleep at 4:30 in the morning, would Barbara wake me up to give me sleeping pills?" he pondered to the audio recording. He talked about the death of her first husband and how he had begun to wonder about its legitimacy. He began to wonder if it had been accidental. And he spoke about her affair.

In the end, Barbara Stager was arrested April 15, 1988 for murder in the first degree of her husband Russell Stager.

Trail and Sentencing

The trial for Barbara Stager concluded on August 30, 1989 with a charge of first-degree murder and a sentence of death.

Barbara's attorney's stressed that she was a devout, churchgoing woman throughout the trial and tried to play on the jury's sympathies. They also indicated that she cooperated fully with law enforcement throughout the whole process and willingly complied with all requests that were made of her. They additionally argued that Barbara was a good mother, a good friend, and an upstanding member of the community. They continued to indicate that she had no criminal record up to this point and there were no mitigating factors to encourage this behaviour. In short, the defence did its job to the best of its ability.

Surprisingly, it was Jason Stager, 14 at the time when he testified about the events of that day, presented a key piece of information in debunking the timeline of his mother's narrative and solidifying her sentence.

He told the court "I was taking a shower when I heard a popping noise. I thought it was the toilet lid dropping. I finished my showed and was getting out when my mother came in and told me that Dad had been hurt. She said I needed to call 911". Jason went on to say he'd been woken up by his alarm clock and then preceded to have a shower.

The timeline presented here varied greatly from what Barbara was saying. Barbara indicated that she had fired the gun at the same time as her son's alarm going off. This testimony came out when the defence called on friends and family to testify to Barbara's good character. Unfortunately, that seemed to backfire on them.

The evidence against Barbara Stager was staggering. The jury deliberated for a grand total of forty-four minutes before they decided on this sentence: guilty.

The sentence of death was changed when it was appealed to a higher court, as all death sentences are, and it was reduced to life in prison. This was due to a technicality in the first hearing. Barbara Stager would be eligible for parole in twenty years as required by the current laws at the time of her sentencing.

Time is Not Enough

In 2009, the first parole date for Barbara Stager rolled around and twenty years was not enough for the town of Durham, North Carolina to forget what had happened to one of its most beloved members. Family members, lawyers, and police officers travelled to the North Carolina Correctional Institute for Women where Barbara Stager had resided for the last twenty years to appeal to the parole board against her release.

"I believe Barbara is a serial killer," Jo Lynn Snow maintains and she maintains that prison is the best place for her.

"She got away with the first one. She thought she could do it a second time, and she didn't make it," said Captain Buchanan. He stands by the fact that Barbara Stager has an evil nature to her. "The former Sunday school teacher has a way of gaining trust that makes her especially dangerous. She's a pillar of the community during the day, but behind closed doors at nigh, she's another woman. She's evil."

Her parole was denied in 2009. Whether this was because of the countless efforts of the family members of Russ Stager, the police involved in the investigation, and the lawyers involved in the case it is difficult to say. Regardless, the parole board did not see it fit to release her back into the public.

Her parole was denied again in 2012 with the parole board making the same decision and her parole hearing was postponed in 2015.

Barbara Stager was up for a new parole hearing on August 1, 2017 and the results of this hearing have yet to hit the media.

BLACK WIDOW : The True Story of DENA THOMPSON

29

BRIANNA WELLS

Dena Thompson is a woman who held power over every man that had the misfortune of falling for her charms.

Dubbed a psychopath, Dena succeeded in fooling everyone around her, including investigators, with her lies and charm for over twenty years.

Dena would post to Lonely Hearts columns and lure a steady stream of lovers and husbands into her world, eventually leaving each one emotionally and financially bankrupt.

Her first husband lost everything to her and wound up as a desperate man on the run from a mafia threat that did not exist. With one husband gone and his money spent, Thompson would go on to bigamously marry Julian Webb, a successful advertising salesman. In three short years, Mr. Webb would be found dead in his bed from an unexplainable drug overdose. Thompson's third and final husband would soon be fighting for his life when she suddenly attacked him with a bat. Still, somehow, this master manipulator would convince an entire jury that she was nothing less than the victim of abuse. No matter how many fruitless chases she sent investigators on, Thompson would not be able to keep the family members and friends of her victims from stringing the pieces together one at a time.

Her crimes were finally brought into the light of day and she would be imprisoned for her killings.

EARLY LIFE

Dena Thompson was born Dena Holmes in 1960 to a lower middle class family from Hendon, London. Her parents were named Michael and Margaret Holmes. Her father had previously worked as a prison officer but had since retired, and her mother lived as a housewife. Her childhood and teenage years held no indication of unhappiness or abuse and she graduated from school with the highest marks. Her life moved by uneventfully until, at the age of 22, she began a career with the Woolwich building society and met Lee Wyatt on a blind date set up by his cousin, Bob Reed, in 1982. On October 12th the following year, the two married in a registry office and moved into a house just below the South Downs. A small village, Dena and Lee's neighbors describe the quaint area as a "very friendly, happy place to live."

Jackie Howells, a neighbor, described the two, saying: "They were ok. You know, just ordinary neighbors when they first moved here."

Pete Howells, Jackie's husband, recalled that Mr. Wyatt was a relatively private man. "Lee kept himself to himself. You know, [polite] enough to say good morning, um, the usual things, but he was never there long enough to build up a conversation with."

Five years later, in 1987, the seemingly happy couple brought a son into the world named Darren.

Lee was an avid toy enthusiast and established the Denalee Crafts company, combining both of their names. The company would distribute hard and soft toys successfully for a time.

For extra income, Dena continued her second job working for the Woolwich building society in Arundel. Taking inspiration from the success of popular cartoon characters and the money behind merchandising, Lee worked to make his fortune by developing a soft toy character for use in cartoon films.

Their shared endeavor would prove not to be the life changing decision they thought it to be, however, when the firm went belly up and Lee was forced to allow his father-in-law to set him up with a new job at the Bedford Hotel in Brighton. Little did Lee know, that this business failure would flip a previously unseen switch in Dena's heart, hurtling her down a dark path of sex, fraud, bigamy, and murder.

Realizing that her seemingly imminent riches were gone before they began, Dena got her first taste of fraud when she began helping herself to the first installments of 26,000 pounds from the Woolwich building society. At the same time, she began to cast her eyes outward for a new man that could bring her success where she felt her current husband had failed. She soon met and began a passionate affair with Julian Webb, whom she met when he visited her office to sell advertising for the West Sussex Gazette.

Julian put forward the idea of doing a makeover using make up and clothing from local businesses in order to bring in customers. At Julian's suggestion, Dena became the model for this idea, and she was very much in love with the new work.

Julian was an active man, an avid bodybuilder and fisherman until he began a relationship with Dena. Soon, his only hobby was to please his new woman.

Peter Howells describes the moment he first saw Dena with Julian , saying: "One day, looking out the back door, [I] just happened to see Dena and another man kissing on the back doorstep, which was rather strange to say the least."

Dena loved the adrenaline rush of both stealing money and cheating on her husband. It was like a drug for her and attaining this kind of "high" would go on to dominate every action she took for the rest of her adult life.

OUT WITH THE OLD, IN WITH THE NEW

Rosemary Webb, Julian's mother, knew very little about Dena when she and Julian came to her with the announcement that they wanted to marry. Understandably, Rosemary was "a bit taken aback at the speed of this, as they'd only met last May," and they had announced their intentions in August of the same year. Only a fortnight later, wedding cards could be seen decorating the front windows of Dena's home. Neighbors were more than a little confused, since Dena Wyatt was already married. No one had seen Lee in weeks and it was as if he disappeared off the face of the earth.

Julian and Dena married on December 2nd, 1991, and Julian did not know that the marriage was bigamous.

Without Julian's knowledge, Dena had sent her first husband running for the hills only months before their marriage. Dena and Lee had signed up for the mortgage on their home together in Yapton, West Sussex. Three months later, in the year of 1991, Denawould give her husband stunning news. She claimed the two needed to separate because Lee was about to come into a large fortune, as there was allegedly a multi-million dollar deal being set up with Walt Disney over his stuffed toy named "Shaun the Leprechaun."

She told him that the mafia was now out to kill him for a cut of the money.

In order to make the lie more believable to Lee, as well as their friends and family, Dena forged letterheads from well-known toy company in the U.S. and showed them to her husband, writing up a lucrative contract that only required his signature.

Lee fell so completely for the deception that he quit his job at the Bedford Hotel.

On June 30th, a debt collector appeared at the door. Dena told her husband to run for his life while she intercepted the man. Lee would run out the back door, praying he would get away unscathed.

Fearing for his family's well-being, Lee Wyatt went on the lamb, but Dena would not allow him to fully disappear without also convincing him to write a series of letters framing himself for the Woolwich building society fraud as she continued to steal more and more money through false accounts.

In an interview taken years later, Lee was quoted saying: "She lives a life of lies and fantasy, and I was the mug who went along with it."

Lee Wyatt gave himself a new name after going on the lamb, Collin Mitchel, and sought work in the Cornish seaside resort of Newquay.

The man that eventually gave him work, David Rodd, was the manager of Carousel Amusements. He stated that Lee came in "to get away from his life in West Sussex, which was nothing strange at the time because a lot of people work for the summer, or something like that." Employees described the mysterious man as easy going and easy to talk to, happy to go out with coworkers for drinks. The job even came with a flat above the establishment that Lee rented for a place to stay. When coworkers eventually learned of his true identity much later, they were more than a little shocked.

A coworker, Mark Pope, laughed about the absurdity of such a sudden revelation, stating in an interview: "Maybe that's why when we were shouting 'Collin' he wasn't replying. We thought he might have been a little bit deaf."

For three years, Lee hid from the invisible boogeymen his cheating wife had created.

Dena, on the other end, set up shop with Julian in the house that Lee had purchased.

Lee sent most of the money he earned to his wife while he lived as a vagrant, believing that any moment his wife would call him, let him know the danger had passed, and finally tell him he could return home to the loving wife and son that awaited him. Dena, however, held no intentions of allowing him to do so, using the money he sent to fund her second wedding and even going so far as to create a gang of fictional assassins called "The G-Men" that were constantly on the hunt for their prey.

Each time Lee called home, praying that at last the "hunt" had been called off, Dena would insist he stay hidden.

Her current beau, Julian, would not be her only suitor during this time as neighbors would recount other men coming in and out of the home while her husband was away at work. There were even a few close calls in which a visitor would be leaving the home almost at the same time as Julian pulled in for lunch, something he did daily.

Christopher Cordess, a legal adviser on Dena Webb's case, had this to say of her: "She has an enormous ability to project, but this is an intense form of it. It had a sort of psychotic flavor, that is a crazy flavor, so intense that it makes people by some extraordinary mechanism -which I can't explain- has an influence over people that makes them do things which their normal selves would never do or do again."

LIES, LIES AND MORE LIES

Early on in her marriage with Julian, Dena informed her husband that she was terminally ill, and that her employer was threatening to fire her because she had taken so many days away from work due to her sickness.

Julian saw this as outrageous as Dena would look the part, acting weak and lethargic. In reality, however, Dena was being fired because 26,000 pounds were missing from accounts at the Woolwich building society, and she was being investigated for it. She claimed that her first husband, Lee, had returned and had been threatening her, blaming him for the missing money. Dena alleged that her first husband was sending her threatening letters and even secretly recorded him making threatening phone calls to her.

Dena then claimed to her neighbors, the Howells, that Lee had come to her home and raped her. The police took her false accusations seriously, and Lee Wyatt finally became the wanted man he had always wrongly believed he was.

Furious of his situation, Lee returned home whilto confront Dena while Julian was upstairs sleeping. Dena refused to explain anything and managed to turn him away. Little did she know that her web of lies had already begun to fall apart at the seams and her subsequent downfall was imminent.

In 1994, Dena took the final step in her downward spiral of darkness: murder. Detectives believe at this time Julian may have begun to discover the extent of his wife's lies before she took his life with a massive overdose of dothiepin, an anti-depressant, and aspirin hidden in his curry over the course of some days.

Julian loved curry with extra spice, a fact that Dena took advantage of to mask the bitter taste of the poison.

It was on Julian Webb's birthday, June 30th, that his devious wife first informed Julian's mother over the phone that her son had fallen ill and had in fact been sick since Tuesday, two days before.

Dena told his mother that her son had "stayed in the sun too long" and had drunk himself into a stupor, which struck his mother as strange.

She knew that her son didn't partake in alcohol.

Friends and work colleagues of Julian had their suspicions as well, as it was very unlike him to be so sick and to not check in with his loved ones. After his second day of missed work, a male co-worker called to inquire if Julian was okay.

"Oh, well, he's sick," Dena said before hanging up on the man. A number of people called the house inquiring after Julian's health, and each caller would receive a vague, fantastic story as to why he could not come to the phone or work.

At 1:30 a.m. in the morning, on Julian's birthday, Dena would ring the doorbell at the Howell residence, waking them.

She told them that she could not wake up her husband and that he was not breathing. When Dena finally called for help, her husband was long dead and rigid in his bed.

Dena presented the police with two bottles, alleging that her husband had taken an overdose of antidepressants and aspirin on purpose. This was a hard pill for his family to swallow, however, as Julian was a fitness fanatic. He never drank or even took aspirin as he was regimented toward clean living.

"I was awake when the police came 'round to tell me what had happened," Julian's mother recalled. "And I knew as soon as I saw them, before I'd spoken to them, and I heard the police car from upstairs. I just knew."

Julian Webb died of an overdose on his 31st birthday in his bed, at least two hours before an ambulance was called.

Julian's coworkers recall coming up to their work building and finding Dena sitting on the front steps a very short time after his death. She was described as moving between crying and lucidity, and the way she seemed to go between the two so quickly unnerved those that witnessed it. Dena is reported to have said in the same breath, "Julian's dead. I need to speak to someone about the insurance money." To any sane person, these two sentences could not possibly be said in the same conversation, much less the same breath, and yet here was this woman wearing a nightgown and jacket, saying just that.

Dena told the police that her husband committed suicide, but his apparent good health and happy attitude prior to his "sickness" prompted police to investigate. They would discover that the antidepressants belonged not to Julian Webb, but to Dena. Still, the pills were kept in a drawer in the kitchen, where Julian could have easily found and taken them, and thus the fact the pills belonged to Dena held little weight. Though the coroner could not confirm that he had taken the dose accidentally, there was not enough evidence to prove foul play so the medical examiner recorded an open verdict.

Wasting no time, Dena attempted to collect thirty-five thousand pounds from Julian's pension plan which was to be released in the event of his death. Julian's mother would not allow her son's murderer to get away with his life and his money, however, and she was able to quickly establish that Dena was not his next of kin as she was still legally married to her first husband.

Dena also attempted to have Julian's remains cremated, but his family and investigators were able to successfully prevent such an evidence damaging act. It would not be until her trial for attempting to murder her third husband, however, that Julian's body would be exhumed.

The funeral was held at a church on Hayling Island in Northney. Dena Webb showed up wearing a high-riding mini-skirt and a blouse that revealed her ample cleavage.

The right side of the church was packed with friends and family mourning the loss of their Julian, and to the left sat the lone figure of Dena in sexy attire. Friends and colleagues describe Dena's face as emotionless and noticed that the flowers she brought appeared to have been taken from the cemetery nearby.

Much to his family's dismay, Julian's death was eventually ruled an accidental overdose, and Dena Webb moved on in her hunt for a new man to take deadly advantage of.

The freshly widowed Dena looked for love by advertising in the personal ads, describing herself as a "bubbly blonde."

No one proved clever enough to resist her charm. Businessmen, teachers, a prison officer, and even a convicted rapist fell under her ruthless spell before she dumped them or vanished. Detectives believe Dena successfully conned her victims out of a total of a half-million pounds.

One of her victims, Robert Waite, was found and interviewed. He had worked with Dena in 1980 and, years later, suddenly received a card from her inviting him to a reunion party. He called her, and Dena invited him to dinner then seduced him.

Dena would tell Waite that Julian had died from an overdose of steroids and that her first husband, Lee Wyatt, had beaten and attacked her regularly. Waite believed her, as he had no reason not to. But when Mr. Waite began to pull away out of disinterest, Dena quickly convinced him that she was dying of a terminal illness. Wishing to help a dying woman, he promised to take her to one of her favorite places, Florida, to care for her during her last months of life. After they arrived, while the two were lying in bed at a motel, Waite woke to feel a sharp prick in his side. He became entirely sure that Dena drugged him and slept through an entire day.

Soon after, Dena left him for broke, saying she had to appear as a witness in an anti-mafia trial in New York. She was actually flying back to Britain as she was due to appear in court for defrauding the Woolwich. For three weeks, Waite was stranded. Evenually, he came back to England and on August 31st, 1995 he discovered that Dena Webb had just been convicted of fraud and sent to jail. It was revealed during this trial that Dena had falsified the alleged death threats sent to her by mail from Lee Wyatt, and even his recorded calls were scripted by her. At the time of their creation, Lee believed that he was creating them to protect his family. The police were able to conclude that Lee was in fact hundreds of miles away during the time of the thefts working in Newquay under an assumed identity, and the charges against him were dropped. Dena was released after only nine months, and she soon returned home.

A NEW MAN, ANOTHER SUCKER

Richard Thompson was just another name on the long list of pockets Dena wished to empty when he discovered her personal ad in a Lonely Hearts column. The two met and "hit it off", marrying in a Holiday Inn in Florida.

The two were forced to round up strangers, one of which was the manager of the hotel, as witnesses after Dena's supposed "friends and family" did not show.

Thompson had money and owned a home in an affluent community which Dena found to her liking. She lied and charmed Thompson, claiming a love of deep-sea fishing which was his favorite hobby.

Dena told Richard that she had won the lottery and could access the money in the States, and so the loving couple made plans to travel overseas and claim her winnings. After the trip had been finalized, Dena enthralled her new husband with ideas of becoming

"a big game ocean skipper" and opening a fishing company.

This inspired Richard to attend classes run by the U.S. Coast Guard. He passed his boating exam, a feat that did not come without a huge amount of hard work. Richard then took an early retirement, and his wife used the money to renovate his cottage in order to rent it out while they were away in Florida building their new life. The new Mrs. Dena Thompson then suggested they combine their financial assets, a suggestion that the blissfully in love Richard saw as a reasonable thing to do. He even made out his will to his wife, giving her power of attorney over his financial affairs. Not long after this, Dena allegedly asked him if their waste disposal unit might be powerful enough to crush bones. A chilling question, to be sure, but a question that Richard thought little about.

Unfortunately for Richard, his wife had a murderous surprise in store for him just one day before the couple were to leave for the States.

On that fateful night, according to Richard's testimony, his wife had promised him a wild round of rough, kinky sex which was something he eagerly accepted.

Before getting ready, Dena locked their German Shepard, Oden, away in another room. She then informed her husband that a man would be coming the following day with a green card for him, which he would then be able to use to go to Florida.

She then started to run a hot bath and told him to "get ready for some fun."

With her husband anticipating something kinky, he allowed Dena to tie up his hands and feet.

"Get ready for a night to remember," she cooed, placing a towel over his face.

Dena then picked up a baseball bat and cracked it over his head.

Once then twice for good measure.

Stunned with blood pouring into his eyes, Richard jerked and twisted his body enough to loosen the restraints on his wrists. He sat up but Dena was ready for him.

Grabbing a butcher knife from the night stand beside their bed, she stabbed him in the shoulder. Still dazed from the baseball bat hits to the head, Richard miraculously recovered and pushed Dena away.

Dena slipped on his blood on the floor. Richard seized the advantage, pushing his thumb into her eye. Dena went for the knife again but Richard pushed harder with his thumb.

"I'll put your eye through your head if you don't let go of the knife," Richard warned.

THE AFTERMATH

It would be several days after Richard fought for and won his life that the idea to check his bank accounts would suddenly come to him. A quick call had his accountant checking his assets, and sure enough, it was discovered that Dena, the woman he had grown to love, had cleaned out his bank accounts. She also made inquiries about surrendering his 89,000 pound life insurance policy and put up his house for sale without his knowledge.

"I fell for her personality," Richard said afterward. "I trusted her 100 percent."

Dena was put on trial for attempted murder and fraud, with Richard as the key witness.

She would plead not guilty and her attorney claimed it was Richard who attacked his wife, becoming violent when she told him that Florida had all been a lie, and that Dena had hit him with the bat in self-defense.

The jury fell for Dena's charm as well, acquitting her of attempted murder.

The district attorney would call the case his "the most staggering court verdict I ever had."

Dena was, however, sentenced to three years and nine months at Lewes Crown Court on fifteen counts of fraud, involving thousands of pounds that she stole from her husband Richard, as well as two other lovers. Not only had Richard been nearly murdered without warning, but now he was financially bankrupt and emotionally devastated. During the trial, Dena admitted that her husband was not the only one she had defrauded, and she was convicted to eighteen months in jail for stealing 26,000 pounds from her old employer, the Woolwich building society, by setting up fake accounts. She had also stolen 5,000 pounds from a former boyfriend.

"I had never seen such a miscarriage of justice," Richard said. "It was appalling."

Dissatisfied with the outcome of the trial, the police began an investigation into Dena's past and quickly discovered some disturbingly repetitive facts. They discovered a long train of men left destitute in the wake of the "bubbly blonde" that promised them love and companionship. They also took a second look at the fate of her late husband, Julian Webb, and the cruel lies that sent Lee Wyatt into homelessness for three years. Immediately following their discovery of Julian Webb's death and the investigation into Dena regarding his overdose, investigators reopened the case and exhumed Julian Webb's body for further examination. For six years, Dena Thompson had gotten away with murder, but the attack on her current husband would prove to be her undoing.

Forensic scientists confirmed that antidepressants caused his death, but concluded that the medication was administered over a period of time rather than all at once. This ruled out Dena's original claim of suicide and made it clear that Julian had in fact been poisoned over the course of a week. Scientists were able to prove this by examining his stomach and blood content. The last days of Julian Webb's life would have been horrific. Isolated from his friends and family, Julian would lie dying in his bed, knowing something was wrong but unable to help himself or reach out to others. All the while, Dena nursed him, likely feeding him by hand in what must have appeared to be an act of love and devotion. Instead, this monstrous psychopath was dosing him with still more and more antidepressants and aspirin.

Julian's final moments would have been filled with agony as his body shut down, with Dena's emotionless face being the last thing he would ever see.

Nine years after his untimely demise, Julian Webb's killer would finally be brought to justice. In 2003, Dena Thompson received life, with a minimum of sixteen years, for murder.

FINALLY...

Dena Thompson was a master manipulator of people, with one husband murdered, another almost murdered, and a third on the run and penniless.

The Recorder of London, Michael Hyam, is quoted saying to Mrs. Thompson that her crimes were "utterly ruthless and without any pity. Nothing can excuse you for the wickedness of what you did."

Immediately after the conviction, UK investigators put together a large scale search for any and all of Mrs. Thompson's previous victims with the fear that they had a serial killer on their hands. The search took investigators and Interpol across the length of Europe to Bulgaria, where Dena had been a regular visitor throughout the late 1970s and early 1980s. One Bulgarian boyfriend by the name of Stoyan Kostov was never found, and the fear is that he was an early victim of Dena who was no referred to as the "Black Widow." How did she make her way to Bulgaria?

Dena was an avid gymnast at a young age, although she never chose to compete, and her father, Michael Holmes, was highly involved in the sport. This is allegedly how Mrs. Thompson's Bulgarian connections were made.

Inspector Martyn Underhill felt a certain sense of urgency when searching for Mr. Kostov (last known address: 27 K.D. Avramov Street, Svishtov), but was unable to find the man.

"We cannot rule out the possibility that other partners have been injured in some way," Inspector Underhill said.

Dena visited Bulgaria for several years, with her gymnastics connections said to be her reason. Much mystery hangs over these visits and the still missing Kostov, and it is suggested that Dena's murderous ways began long before she ever met Julian Webb. If Kostov is indeed Dena Thompson's first victim, he could be the only person on earth capable of shedding light on what turned Dena towards a life of crime.

The investigation came to an eventual end, however, when no solid evidence could be found on any murders prior to Julian Webb. Some, including a UK journalist named Adrian Gatton, believe that there is much more to the Bulgarian story than could be found by police. It is suggested that the operation carried out by Interpol and West Yorkshire police was done half-heartedly, as they may never have visited Bulgaria.

There are likely many unnamed men made victims by Dena Thompson's grandiose lies, but they might feel too embarrassed to come forward and identify themselves. It is proven that she stole from a dozen different men, but police believe the number to be much larger. Dena Thompson maintains her innocence, and her most recent appeal against conviction has failed.

In 2007, she was sentenced to a minimum of sixteen years in prison.

GOLD DIGGER VIRGINIA LARZELERE

SAMANTHA RUE

Virginia Larzelere: Incarcerated and spared the electric chair

Mid-afternoon shots rang out in the middle of a suburban dental clinic almost 27 years ago. A frantic call was received by emergency dispatch. The call was made by the wife of the slain dentist yelling down the line for assistance to save her husband's life, following a fatal gunshot wound to the chest.

March 8, 1991 was the day that changed Virginia Larzelere's life forever. The cold-blooded murder of her dentist husband Norman Larzelere sparked off a chain of events that culminated in her lifelong incarceration. Although it could be proven that she never pulled the trigger on her husband, the prosecution successfully argued that she was the mastermind behind the crime. Police investigating the crime scene discovered that as Norman lay dying in a pool of blood he mumbled, "Was that Jason?"

Jason was his son, adopted when he had married Jason's mother.

The investigation would result in a bizarre set of confessions that implicated Virginia Larzelere in the murder for money case. Psychiatric and hearsay evidence pointed to the motive of death to be avarice and a psychopathic manipulation of men throughout her life. Although Virginia's death sentence was commuted to life in 2008, she asserts she is still innocent to this day.

The Crime: Murder at midday, March 8, 1991

The masked killer silently entered through the back door of the dentist's surgery, with a sawed-off shotgun held by his side. His mission was to kill Norman Larzelere, possibly for the life insurance money in some sort of deal with Virginia. The sound of footsteps alarmed Norman as he had not heard anyone enter through the door.

During the trial, Dr Larzelere was reported to have said, "Who's there?" The other occupants of the office at the time were his wife Virginia and the state's witness, Kristen Palmieri who barely looked up when Norman went into the corridor to find out what the disturbance was.

Testimony provided in the first murder hearing alleged that upon seeing a gunman in the shady office corridor, he yelled, "No!" and ran back into the office slamming his office door behind him. The gunman who was in close pursuit was able to pull the trigger once, shattering through the door and hitting the doctor's chest. He subsequently died at the scene from a combination of chest trauma causing a pneumothorax (collapsed lung) and fatal blood loss.

His wife, Virginia, rushed to his side and yelled for someone to call 911. The report from the ambulance dispatcher subsequently reported that Virginia yelled to the 911 dispatcher, "Someone just came in and shot my husband! Somebody shot my husband!"

As Norman's life seeped away, she cradled him, crying. The witness alleged that he asked Virginia, "Where's Jason? Was that Jason?" By the time the police and ambulance had arrived, the gunman had fled, leaving behind a trail of devastation and turmoil. Just as he had sneaked into the clinic without being detected that fateful afternoon, as he was able to leave with none of the witnesses able to positively identify him.

The question, "Was that Jason?" uttered by the dying man, formed the basis of an investigation, where the prosecution's case pinning the murder of Dr Norman Larzelere on Virginia's biological son, Jason.

Betrayal, Lies, Manipulation

Piecing together the various players in this shocking murder for money was the task of Detective Dave Gamell. His first major lead came from the confession of Steve Heidle who had called the detective in May to reveal his hand at disposing of the murder weapon. He claimed that he had been directed by Virginia to clean the weapon in muriatic acid and then bury it in concrete.

Heidle claimed that he was aided in his endeavours by the witness Kristen Palmieri, who like himself, was employed by the slain victim's wife, Virginia Larzelere. Both of them gave statements saying that Virginia had blackmailed them into doing terrible things. Heidle also confessed to knowing about a plan to kill Norman for his life insurance and he alleged that she paid her son Jason $200,000 to kill his adopted father and benefactor.

Heidle, like many others that were unveiled during the investigation, was used as a pawn of Virginia Palmieri to assist in the hiding of evidence. Heidle spent hours with Gamell and provided a lot of useful evidence, not just about disposing the weapons but also about the family dynamics at play that led to the murder being committed by Jason.

According to the state prosecutors, the main motive for killing the well-respected and loved dentist was to bank the payout from Norman's recent increase in life insurance, which had been in place just prior to his untimely death.

Heidle claimed that Virginia had an insatiable appetite for men and money. He also claimed she lived a life filled with drugs and crime all of which made him intimidated to stand up to her. He told Detective Gamell, that if she could get her husband killed in broad daylight, then he feared for his own life if he did not do as instructed. He agreed to hide the evidence and buried the gun deep in the waters of Pellicer Creek.

That same afternoon following Heidle's confession, Kristen Palmieri was called for questioning. She corroborated Heidle's account of the events, telling the detective that she knew that hiding the weapons was wrong. She said that she had never believed that Jason could have been the murderer but subsequently Jason had confessed to her that he had been forced to kill his father at Virginia's behest.

Sure enough, police divers uncovered a plastic container with a rusted shotgun embedded in concrete in Pellicer Creek. In exchange for turning state's witness, Heidle and Palmieri were granted immunity from further prosecution.

Following this significant piece of evidence, Virginia Larzelere was caught and arrested by police the following day. It was said she was attempting to flee from Edgewater with a lot of cash and jewellery in her purse. Detective Gamell had years of experience in homicide investigations and claims he could detect her fake mourning. "I've dealt with a lot of murders and a lot of deaths," Gamell said. "And you know when someone mourns legitimately and when someone's overacting. That's how she seemed."

Gold Digging and Incest: the prosecution's case

As the state's case against Jason and his mother unfolded, it was Heidle's statements to police that provided ample motive for the crime. Heidle claimed that he'd overheard a conversation between Jason and Virginia where she had said that she'd increased the life insurance policy and forged his signature. Dr Larzelere had no suspicions of his wife's dark intentions. Heidle's sworn statement reads, "She said she's [forged] all of Norman's legal documents and it was no big deal." Evidence presented in court revealed that prior to the murder, there had been an increase on the value of the life insurance from $1 million to $2.1 million. Furthermore, a few weeks before the murder, it appeared that his will had been amended to favor his wife. Previously, she was not listed as a sole benefactor.

The trial was a field day for sensationalist journalists who reported on the case. There were many scandalous angles to report. Virginia had already been involved in an embezzlement scheme some years before. Although the charges had been dropped, it was clear that the many people in her life (such as the key witness Heidle) did not like her. It was argued that Virginia was a heartless gold digger who had a long history of manipulating all the men in her life in order to get better resources and status.

While Norman had been dearly loved in Edgewater, it was the belief of many in the small town, that Virginia's arrival in his life was a targeted and calculated move by her. She was a ruthless femme fatale who saw the married dentist as an easy mark. Norman had divorced his wife soon after beginning an affair with Virginia and they married within two months of the divorce being finalized.

Heidle was the key witness and he gave evidence throughout the trial of many instances that implicated Virginia with the murder. Allegations were that Norman Larzelere's life insurance policy and will were forged were denied by Larzelere's defence attorney, Jack Wilkins.

Wilkins was an attorney who loved representing members of the rich party crowd to which Virginia belonged. He claimed that it was great to represent this echelon of drug-taking socialites, as they always paid in cash. Wilkins seemed more like *Breaking Bad's* Saul Goodman, flamboyantly representing drug dealers and winning on minor technicalities.

Wilkins was more a party boy than a lawyer, and while he did have credibility in winning some prominent cases, he lacked the experience to deal with serious forensic evidence. Although he won a prominent civil rights case permitting a small town cinema to sell pornographic movies, he was simply out of his depth in a murder trial.

Virginia's poor choice of lawyer was to seal her fate. Wilkins was a dreadful choice to represent her as he'd admitted, "I'd never done a capital murder case before." During Larzelere's appeal case, evidence was tendered to the court to show that Wilkins had a very serious substance abuse problem, with daily use of vodka, cocaine and methamphetamines. Wilkins did try to turn down the case, but Virginia insisted on retaining him.

The relatively inexperienced and often inebriated Wilkins had to go up against the surgical-like precision of Special Prosecutor Dorothy

Sedgwick's argumentative style. Appointed by the District Attorney, Sedgwick was chosen for her assassin-like instincts to win at all costs. She ran a vicious case against Virginia calling into question the background of the accused.

It was only in the subsequent appeal hearings against the death sentence that many important facts about Virginia's early life were brought to light. Much of the blame for this apparent miscarriage of proper judicial process can be laid at Wilkins' feet. Even Sedgwick was on the record commenting that a decent defence lawyer would have called witnesses to refute some of the state's evidence. Wilkins never sought the opinion of a psychiatrist nor any other expert to take the stand on Virginia's behalf.

The multi-generational level of neglect and sexual misconduct towards children was the key to the prosecution case. Court reports show that under psychiatric questioning, it was clear that as a child growing up, Virginia believed that sexual behavior with family members was the norm. This allowed the prosecutor to paint Virginia as a ruthless killer. In other words, if she was a murderer, being an incestuous murderer made it all the more salacious and perhaps believable to the jury who ultimately convicted her of the murder of Dr Norman Larzelere.

Under Sedgwick's direction, the jury was directed to focus on Virginia's apparently insatiable appetite for men and money as the primary motivation for the murder plot. Sedgwick presented psychiatric evidence to prove that Virginia had a personality disorder which caused her pathological love of money and control.

In the trial, Virginia was successfully portrayed as a manipulative woman with psychopathic tendencies who seduced her son Jason to murder his father, in order to benefit from the life insurance claim. She then used money and blackmail to gain the loyalty of people such as Heidle and Palmieri and her own children.

The state was unable to convict Jason and he was acquitted in 1992 as there was insufficient evidence to place him at the scene of the crime that fateful March day in 1991. However Virginia's guilty verdict and death sentence stayed. It was always clear that she did not murder her husband by her own hand, but suspicions remain as to her collusion due to the circumstantial evidence

How did it come to this?

Virginia grew up in the 1950s in a small town called Lake Wales, 60 miles south of Orlando, Florida. She was the oldest of four daughters all living with their Mom and Dad in a three bedroom bungalow in the working class part of the town. Both of her parents worked in a local juice company called Donald Duck.

Dr Mosman, the psychiatrist giving evidence in the appeal case told the court that she had confided to him that her father, "Pee-Wee" Antley, was a strong dictator whose moods ruled the house of women. It was noted he was a huge drinker who sexually abused each of his daughters (and subsequently Virginia's own children Jessica and Jason). In an interview with the Miami New Times in 2013, Virginia said, "sexual abuse doesn't only happen in poor households, does it?"

Virginia's younger sister, Peggy, testified that Virginia took more of the sexual abuse from their father in an attempt to spare her younger sisters. The abuse would gave birth to a burden of silence, of not being able to confide in people outside the family or to get any help for them or their mother. Mosman revealed to the court that the father was, "a chronic alcoholic, sitting on the porch drinking daily, with no outside hobby or social interests."

Virginia left home at the age of seventeen but the scars of abuse never left. Having been a victim of abuse from as young as the age of three, the emotional and sexual trauma stayed with her and influenced her outlook on life and on men. Virginia knew that the best way to survive was to use men to gain access to the wealth that she needed to feel free from her demons.

Her success at attracting many men (she was married three times by the time she was in her early 30s) came about because she was able to use her looks and sexual conduct to acquire goods and status throughout her life. Even Virginia's daughter Jessica (from her first marriage to Harry Mathis), said that the child abuse she had suffered led her to be ruthless and impulsive. Jessica has stated in an interview some years ago that, 'My mother is a very intelligent woman, who had looks which she used to her advantage." The state's case relied on this aspect of her love of the high life and of sexual promiscuity to draw the sketch of her as a ruthless gold-digging murderer.

The entire prosecution case was based on Heidle's voluntary testimony, which painted Virginia as the product of a dysfunctional and incestuous family. It was alleged that her exposure to serious childhood abuse and trauma led to her manipulative and ruthless tendencies. However, no psychiatrist was ever called by the defence to undertake an evaluation of her mental state.

Virginia's teen marriage

In Lake Wales where Virginia was growing up, she did not have any friends. This is because her domineering father felt the need to protect his filthy secret from authorities so visitors were restricted from visiting the home.

Virginia attended and graduated from Lake Wales High school and immediately fled home to marry Harry Mathis when she was only 17 years old. Soon after the marriage, she fell pregnant with Jason and then Jessica. Experts say that people often people who have dysfunctional parents often choose dysfunctional partners, and this certainly appears to be the case with Virginia.

She was trapped as a young mom, from a dysfunctional background now living with an abusive husband. Harry Mathis beat his wife and son Jason, as evidenced in the police records. Virginia divorced him in 1978, determined to be as far away from his abuse as possible, and wanting a new life for her two young children, Jason and Jessica. Instead of seeing her getting away from Harry as a triumph against abuse, the prosecutor used this to demonstrate that Virginia 'burned through' husbands. The prosecutor even used the fact that she wished for her abusive ex-huband's death as evidence of her murderous intent for Norman.

However, despite the various setbacks, abuse and domestic violence there remained in Virginia evidence of a clear determination to not only survive but thrive. Once she had escaped her parental home of horror, she went into another dysfunctional marriage for a brief period. It is also a fact that she had turned to substances to numb the emotional pain from a young lifetime of abuse. She was clearly not the most stable woman in Edgewater, but she was a survivor.

Leaving Mathis started her love of freedom, and of the partying good life that has been portrayed through documentaries about the case.

Socialite in the making

Having been divorced at the age of 25, and with two young children in tow, Virginia was clearly on a mission to find a man that would replace their biological father as a role model in her life. Being denied a good role model of appropriate masculinity, she was easily distracted by the promises of various men simply looking for a woman to bed. However, she was also hungry for money and status but preferred freedom to being tied to a man It appears that her main goal since leaving home at 17 had been to free herself from the control of a man.

Her hunger for a better life, even being married three times before she was 32, demonstrates a decision to turn away from the cycle of abuse that her mother had endured. Virginia's mother stayed by her husband's side through the mistreatment and abuse of all of his daughters. In a sense, her mother colluded with him by permitting the abuse to be perpetuated, child after child. Her misplaced loyalty for, and fear of, her husband kept her at his side.

Virginia's drive to be different from her passive mother showed her adventurous spirit, her impulsiveness and her keen business sense. By the mid-1980's she had worked her way up to being the president of a construction company based in the little town of Edgewater, a seaside town, two hours north of her hometown, Lake Wales. Although Edgewater was still a very small and isolated town, she had successfully changed her fortunes. Her financial success had become like a drug It made her feel good, and the more she did of it, the better she felt.

Her stars changed completely in 1985 due to the happenstance of a dental appointment where she was to meet the love of her life. It was in Dr Norman Larzelere's dental surgery that love was born. Virginia claims that from that first meeting she knew he was 'the one'. The feelings were clearly mutual, as the already married dentist quickly divorced his wife so that he could make a life for Virginia and her children. He embraced Jason and Jessica as his own and officially adopted them when they married.

"There was nothing but love in that household," fhe family's housekeeper Juanita Washington said. "Nothing but love." Upon their marriage, the newlyweds Virginia and Norman promptly moved into a mansion in a prestigious uptown area. The home had previously housed all sorts of people from the higher echelons of society including congressional representatives and bank presidents. By all accounts, despite the differences in their social standings and backgrounds, they seemed to be deliriously happy and to be true soul mates.

Storm clouds over paradise

However, things started to get a bit difficult the following year as Virginia's business went bankrupt amid allegations of embezzlement. Settling out of court, all criminal charges were dismissed. Around this time, her teenage son Jason was getting a bit out of hand, as teenagers in blended families often do.

Jason was a known party boy in the local Orlando gay club scene. He also befriended drag queens and seemed to have inherited his biological father's love of beating women."He threw me down the stairs and broke my ribs by kicking me over and over again," his sister Jessica recalled. "I had told my dad that Mom was cheating on him with a patient of his." Jason staunchly defended his mother and allegations of her sexual appetites together with her son's strong filial devotion was a source of gossip surrounding their potentially incestuous relationship.

Virginia never denied her sexual liaisons with several men, two of whom testified that she had asked them to 'get rid' of Norman. It was clear that whatever their relationship was in public, Norman was unable to control his headstrong and hard-partying wife. Some of the testimonies only came to light when these men of low character asked to be paid to testify, making them barely credible.

No friends to testify on Virginia's behalf

With the public salivating upon every salacious fact, it was fair to say that Virginia and Jason Larzelere were convicted in the court of public opinion before the jury delivered its 5-7 guilty verdict for Virginia. Jason was subsequently acquitted due to the flimsy evidence by a disgruntled employee (Heidle) being the sole evidence in the case. Subsequent hearings brought to light the fact that the lone gunman that fateful day was not Jason, as Heidle had conveniently framed him for the murder. As Heidle had been given immunity from prosecution, many speculate that he tainted the stories about Virginia to protect himself and that it was he who murdered Larzelere. He committed suicide in 1999.

The allegations that Virginia was the mastermind who had her husband killed in cold blood to collect on his significant life insurance were presented but never successfully refuted. Her defence lawyer did not call any witness to the stand to testify on her behalf. A lifetime of alienation from meaningful relationships robbed her of this comfort. Her childhood of abuse and neglect impaired her ability to make and sustain meaningful and enduring friendships.

Her death sentence was overturned in 2008 though she remains incarcerated in the Homestead Correctional Institution, a 65-year-old widow, and she still maintains her innocence.

BLACK WIDOW BETTY LOU BEETS

ALICE WATERS

Betty Lou Beets is a perfect historical example of how multifaceted crime can be, how a victim could become an aggressor, or an aggressor may adopt the mask of victimhood, and how all is not necessarily as it seems. Convicted for murdering two men and assaulting or attempting to kill four, Betty Lou's story is one that would send chills down the spine of any man from any era. Only the fourth woman to be executed for murder, despite the overall statistics hovering around forty to fifty cases of capital punishment per year, her crimes were too gruesome and cold for the court to offer her a lesser sentence... or were they? As we shall see when we delve into her history, despite Betty Lou's extensive criminal record and constant charges against her from ex husbands and her own children, the justice system was eager to give her a way out of the death sentence and allow her to live her natural life out in prison. And although there were some mitigating circumstances, it is telling that Betty Lou Beets almost got away with a life sentence in a situation where many others would have been executed without remorse.

Betty Lou Beets was born Betty Lou Dunevant on the 12th of March 1937, in Roxboro, North Carolina, USA. Her parents were initially tobacco farmers, whose main pleasure in life was alcohol, resulting in rampant alcoholism and a violent family life not atypical of the rural poor of the Great Depression. They lived on a diet of salt pork and various flours, barely touching vegetables or fruit, let alone eggs, fish, nuts or pulses, essential for developing a healthy brain and body. Furthermore, Betty Lou was disabled. She was not completely deaf, but hard of hearing due to having contracted the measles some time between the ages of three and six. Her fever was so severe and prolonged that she suffered damage to her brain and ears. As her hearing was affected at such a young age, she suffered an impairment to her speech similar to what many deaf or hard of hearing children suffer. At another time, or in another family, Betty Lou may have received treatment and hearing aids, but as a poor family in 1940, they could not afford to get her the treatment she would have needed to hear and speak normally. Her education was strongly impacted as she could not learn to read or study, resulting in borderline illiteracy and innumeracy and a frustrating life at home and away. Betty Lou also claimed she had been raped by her father in early childhood, as well as sexually abused by others. By the age of twelve her family life was falling apart. Her mother had been institutionalized due to breakdowns caused by alcoholism and Betty Lou had to drop out of school so she could care for her younger brother and sister. Her father, who seemed to see her as a surrogate mother for her siblings, became guarded against any sign of Betty Lou escaping and would beat her for not taking full responsibility for her siblings. She was often at the doctor's office or in hospital for the injuries he inflicted on her. She finally left school completely. The family moved to Hampton, Virginia, while Betty Lou was still a young girl, so that her father could work as a machinist. They were poor, she was young and disabled and she was a victim at the hands of the very people who were supposed to care for her. These circumstances were hardly the healthiest for the young girl to grow up in, and it is not shocking that Betty Lou became increasingly unstable and inclined to criminality in such an environment during such a time of deprivation. However it is also noteworthy that many more people suffered equal or worse hardship, yet did not turn to criminal activity. Perhaps it was the combination of everything, all together at once, but as she grew up something was going very, very wrong inside Betty Lou.

At the age of fifteen she married her first husband, Robert Franklin Branson. Far from an age where anyone feels quite ready to move into adulthood, Betty Lou was married for the first time. She would remain with him for seventeen years before finally divorcing. Although she levied accusations of violence against all her husbands, Robert Franklin Branson was the only one whose life she did not threaten directly herself. It appears he picked up where her father left off. If she was ever a unilateral victim, this may have been the one time. Within the first year she attempted suicide and became pregnant. They had a daughter together. She also later had a son with Robert Branson, who was also named Robert after his father. They went onto have four more children. Their children may have been a factor in reducing the marital violence, extending the duration of the relationship and, ultimately, saving Robert Branson Senior's life. In 1958 he evicted her from their home and put her on a bus to Virginia while he kept her children, at which point Betty again attempted suicide via an overdose of sleeping pills. They divorced in 1969, which left Betty Lou a financial and emotional wreck.

Being single took its toll on Betty Lou. She attached her self-worth to her ability to stay married. She began drinking to fight her feelings of loneliness. Between her own insecurities and the hard time she had getting money from either Robert Branson or the Welfare service to support her, Betty Lou soon felt she needed to remarry. She married Billy York Lane at the age of thirty two. Their marriage was a tumultuous one, and very short. There was evidence of mutual violence and disregard for each other's wellbeing. Lane had been abusive towards a previous partner and Betty Lou responded to his violence in turn. Her daughters recall how he used to beat her senseless and how she used to attack him. He initially wanted to charge her for attempted murder, but swiftly dropped the charges after he was forced to admit he had attacked her, broken her nose and threatened her life. They divorced the same year and remarried again shortly after the trial.

After Betty Lou shot at him, Billy York Lane divorced her again, only a month after their remarriage, this time for good. It would prove the wisest decision of his life, as her subsequent husbands found out.

Betty Lou remained single for a year and unmarried for eight more years. During the interim Betty Lou worked in a warehouse, then took up work at a topless bar to cover the bills. She sent two of their children back home to Branson, as she could not afford to care for them. She went on to marry Ronnie C. Threlkold, her boyfriend of seven years, at the age of forty. However this relationship would be as unpredictable, violent and dangerous for Ronnie as it was for Billy. In this case there was little evidence Ronnie had been violent towards Betty Lou, although she accused him of violence at later dates, but her habits had been firmly cemented and she continued to display abusive behaviour towards him. She also continued to work at the topless bar, resulting in arrests and thirty days in country jail under the charge of public lewdness. Despite their seven year courtship, the marriage lasted just a year, culminating in Betty Lou Beets's attempted homicide of Ronnie in 1978, where she shot him in the stomach, wounding him, and their divorce in 1979.

She married Doyle Wayne Barker at the age of forty one, closely after her divorce from Threlkold. Their marriage lasted a mere seven weeks before her violent behaviour drove Doyle away from her. However his own violence was undeniable. He had stalked her, assaulted her and raped her during their short relationship. The day he left Betty Lou had bruises all over her face, neck, arms and chest. There is no available record of the divorce, however all living parties assumed it had taken place. However Doyle Wayne did not get out of their marriage unscathed. He disappeared after their divorce and his body was found years later, buried under a garage, killed by three gunshots.

But this grisly deed was not uncovered for many more years to come. Rather, Betty Lou went on to marry a firefighter named Jimmy Don Beets, her final husband, at the age of forty four.

"Jimmy Don Beets was a wonderful man," said a family friend. "He was loved by so many people. An old country boy that a lot people had respect for."

Their courtship would last a mere six months. Betty Lou would meet Jimmy while she worked as a waitress and the seduction began. Her two sons moved in with them. This would be her final marriage, and her actions within it would be her undoing. Although their courtship had been pleasant, they both suffered from alcoholism, which slowly drove their marriage to the same violence she had experienced previously. Less than a year later she murdered him by gunshot, and this time she was caught. Robert Branson, her son from her first marriage, had been informed that she intended to kill her last husband, telling him to steer clear of the residence as the murder took place. On the 6th of August 1983, Robert Branson Junior left their home and Betty Lou Beets committed the gruesome act. Not only did Robert provide evidence that the act was premeditated, but he also was expected to participate. Two hours after leaving the house, Robert Branson Junior returned, finding his step father dead with two gunshot wounds in his body. Rather than seek assistance, Robert Branson Junior, either tainted by a lifetime with a mother who viewed abuse and murder as daily events or himself an individual with low empathy, helped his mother to dispose of the body. Betty Lou Beets and Robert Branson Junior carted Jimmy Don Beets' body outside to an ornamental wishing well that stood in the front yard of their house. Undetected, they cast the body inside.

Then, Betty Lou returned to the house to cover up her acts. She called the police to report her husband missing from their Cedar Creek Lake home. The next day, Betty Lou became more devious. Perhaps inspired, perhaps unnerved by her success killing Doyle Wayne Barker, she realized she needed to create a story with which to divert the police from her trail. Robert Branson Junior recalled to the press how she had taken some of Jimmy Don Beets's heart medication down to his boat at the lake. Then she had removed the propeller, placed the medication in the boat and abandoned it, floating loosely in the water. Later that day, as the twenty four hours since Jimmy Don Beets's initial disappearance drew to a close, various officials began the search for the presumably missing man. Officers from the Henderson County Sheriff's department, various members of the fire department, as well as agents from the Texas Parks and Wildlife department searched for three weeks. They naturally found no body. However they did find Jimmy Don Beets's boat drifting in the lake, near to the Redwood Beach Marina. There they found his fishing license, an unused life jacket and the heart medication which Betty Lou Beets had placed there. Not knowing anything about the murder or the forged evidence, they brought Betty Lou Beets to the Marina as the sole witness, where she identified the boat and its contents as those of her husband. Although no body had been recovered, it was considered case closed.

Betty Lou Beets would have likely got away with both murders, were it not for confidential information given to the Henderson County Sheriff's Department two years later. The information suggested that Jimmy Don Beets had not disappeared innocently, and that his assumed death, with no body that had been found, may be the result of foul play. The evidence was enough that the cold case was reopened in Spring 1985. As their suspicions became stronger, the investigators were drawn to Betty Lou Beets, who was arrested on the 8th of June of 1985 and then booked into the Henderson County Jail. An officer on the case, Rick Rose, who had been in charge of her arrest warrant, secured a further warrant to search the Beets's home and lands, including the yard. Ultimately, they discovered Jimmy Don Beets's remains buried under the wishing well where he had been left two years prior. But another discovery would surface that would further disturb the case. Also in the back yard was a storage shed which could be moved. When the officers moved it, something compelled them to disturb the soil that had lain there several years. Perhaps it was some confidential evidence or perhaps it was just intuition, but it paid off when they discovered a second body. Doyle Wayne Barker, still missing, was buried there, with three bullets in his body. All five bullets matched the .38 caliber pistol which had been seized from their home after another incident of Betty Lou's violent outbursts. Thanks to the calls she had made the very day of his disappearance there was no room to argue that she had been abusing drugs or alcohol at the time, but there had been no physical evidence that suggested to detectives at the time that Jimmy Don had been abusing her when the incident took place. Her position was weak.

Faced with the evidence, Robert Branson Junior and his sister Shirley finally confessed to their awareness of the killings, as well as their hand in the crimes that had taken place. Not only had Betty Lou told her son about the murder, but she had also informed her daughter, by the Shirley Stegner and not living at the family home, that she planned on killing her husband. Shirley was motivated by her confession to also confess to her involvement in another crime. She told the detectives that she had been involved in the burial of Doyle Wayne Barker's body in October of 1981 after Betty Lou had shot him to death.

In an effort to make herself more likeable to the jury, Betty Lou Beets raised her history of domestic violence as an excuse for her violent behaviour, levying charges against all her prior husbands, as well as her father. However, this would be the first that anyone had heard of most of these charges. This may have been due to attitudes of the times, a desire to protect her children, or the apparently two-sided nature of most of these incidents, however the jury would not believe her claims. They were just too convenient. Instead, it was clear to them that Betty Lou Beets was an unstable and dangerous woman and the only connection between the five men she married and their violence. Whatever the situation was, her psychological well being was never considered during the trial. Despite the obvious impact her upbringing and life would have on her mental state and the fact that her actions up until that point were indicative of definite mental illness, the trial system of the time did not account for that.

Furthermore, the premeditated nature of her actions was evident through her children's abundant testimonials, where they confessed she had shared her intent to kill not only the husbands she managed to murder, but that she had expressed a desire to kill all the men she had been married to. Not only that, but her success concealing the bodies, under the wishing well and under the garden shed, showed a lack of remorse and serious consideration of her crimes. However it seems Betty Lou had not been as careful as she thought. As soon as the trial began, various other witnesses emerged to testify against her. Various people recalled her attempting to collect life insurance of over a hundred thousand dollars as well as a pension of over a thousand dollars a month after Jimmy Don's declared death. A year after the official death of Jimmy Don Beets, she successfully sold his boat, the primary evidence that he had disappeared. She claimed she did not know about his pension or insurance, however seeing as Jimmy Don Beets was already retired and claiming his pension, this claim fell short. Furthermore, had she no awareness of them she would not have pursued either so actively. She claimed she had been told about them when she visited an attorney by the name or E. Ray Andrews about a fire insurance claim she needed to make, at which point he discovered she could claim his insurance and pension. However her own filing for these benefits did not align with the supposed visit, and the only person who could say for sure that she had not known about her deceased husband's finances was E. Ray Andrews himself, who agreed to represent her in exchange for the rights to book and movie deals concerning her life and case.

Betty Lou Beets was indicted for murder for remuneration or the promise of remuneration, with her recovery of his life insurance and pension as evidence. She plead not guilty and was taken to trial, where she was found guilty of the capital offence of first degree murder on the 11th of October of 1985. She was found again guilty during a hearing on the 14th of October 1985 and was sentenced to death by the trial court. This was due to her prior history of violence and attempted murders, which suggested that she would present a threat to others in the future, specifically to any man who entered a relationship with her again. Yet her conviction and sentence were quickly and successfully appealed to the Texas Court of Criminal Appeals. Such was the situation that, under Texas law, crime for the sake of insurance and pension claims was not covered by the definition of "murder for remuneration", instead falling into two separate categories of first degree murder and insurance fraud, or crime with intent to commit insurance fraud. The Texas Court of Criminal Appeals reversed her conviction for capital murder, citing the Texas Penal Code as evidence that her particular case could not be filed as "murder for remuneration". The State then requested a rehearing of the cause. Although her original conviction had been overturned, the fact remained that Betty Lou Beets was guilty of homicide under some circumstance or another.

On the 21st of September of 1988, the Court of Criminal Appeals reinstated her conviction and sentence based on the evidence received. Betty Lou Beets was on death row. Her execution was scheduled for the 8th of November 1989.

However her court case did not go as it should have in the first place. Attorney E. Ray Andrews was heavily invested in sensationalizing her case as much as he could, seeing as he would profit enormously from the case blowing up into a media phenomenon. So although she claimed and he later agreed that she had known nothing of her husband's finances, the trial was conducted under the assumption that she was fully aware of the money she would receive. Not only that, but E. Ray Andrews did everything in his power to create a more dramatic case on both sides, which ultimately meant excluding Betty Lou from much of the information about her own trial. Betty Lou was becoming desperate at this point. Although she had a long history of domestic violence, attempted murder and two bodies in her garden, she decided to attempt to blame the murder of Jimmy Don Beets on Robert Branson Junior, her own son. She did not seem to have made the statement in sound mind, but E. Ray Andrews allowed her to speak on her own behalf and did not retract it, as it added dramatic quality to the event. He tried to cover up later, saying that Betty Lou had possibly been taking the blame for her son, however he had no proof other than that Robert Branson Junior was male and from a rough background. This statement and its acceptance horrified the court, as it was alarming to them to see a mother who, rather than protect her children, was willing to throw them under the bus by falsely accusing them of a crime she had more than evidently committed. Furthermore, by admitting and adhering to the story that Robert Branson Junior was in fact the actual killer, Betty Lou lost all chances of arguing that she acted in self-defence and made her own accusations of domestic violence against Jimmy Don and her prior husbands completely irrelevant. This is despite the fact that a leading domestic violence specialist of the time believed Betty Lou Beets had been significantly mentally impacted by her experiences, and that she suffered "the emotional, cognitive, and behavioural components of battered woman syndrome, rape trauma syndrome, and PTSD" which he added must have interacted with her pre-existing organic brain damage from her childhood illness, history of battering and substance abuse. All together, this would have presented a robust case for her mental illness and need for treatment rather than punishment. However E. Ray Andrews discarded this option in favour of the more dramatic choice of supporting Betty Lou's accusation against her son. They became stuck in the position of having to argue she did not kill her husband at all. This context may have reduced her sentence, or made her eligible to claim insanity. However neither of these options were available.

Throughout the entire case, E. Ray Andrews failed to represent her seriously and did nothing to prevent her from shooting herself in the foot repeatedly. In fact, seeing the case was a lost cause and that he stood to gain more from her sentence than her freedom, Andrews began drinking heavily for the duration of the trial. He chose not to bear witness to her claims that she did not know about Jimmy Don Beets's pension or insurance, which would have transformed the case to one of murder in the context of domestic violence, rather than murder for remuneration. He managed to offer the jury no reasons to consider that Betty Lou was not a serious threat to those around her, eventually sealing her fate. Yet he remained her attorney for the duration of her appeal as well. It was he who raised the point that her financial gain was not necessarily the motivator for murder, but a by product. He also finally raised that she was not aware of the insurance or pension until she spoke to him, however this was met with scepticism due to his negligence to mention it any sooner, and was perceived as a lie in effort to overturn Betty Lou's criminal charges after his initial failure to protect her.

On the 16th of October 1989, Betty Lou filed a motion called a stay of execution which would delay her execution to give her time to prepare and file a habeas corpus application with the state. On the 1st of November she filed the application and the trial court delayed her execution so that the claims she was raising, such as consideration towards her mental state and marital conditions, could be properly addressed. During this time Betty Lou wrote several letters from prison in which she attempted to defend her good name and that of her last husband. She attempted to balance the accusations that she was a black widow by reminding the court that she was Jimmy Don's fourth wife as well. However his previous wives did not come forward to support her. She also defended her own identity, denying that she ever worked as a barmaid, regardless of her own charges for lewd behaviour, and that she was never on welfare, despite her claims after her first divorce. She also said that the Fire Department Chaplain, who stated he had informed her about Beets's insurance and pension, had spoken to her sister in law, Betty Beets, instead. She even quibbled over the descriptions of her garden, insisting the well was a planter in the shape of a well and not an actual well. It was clear that Betty Lou Beets was desperate to save face and project a more pleasant, more ordinary identity than the one which E. Ray Andrews had created for her in the courtroom. It was also clear that her mental health was degrading as she endured life in prison and submitted her habeas corpus petition. In her petition she argued against her sentence of the death penalty, raising issues such as the alleged value Jimmy Don Beets apparently added the community, the testimonials of victims and sufferers whose statements were unconstitutional under the Victim Impact Statements act of 1987, and the poor assistance which E. Ray Andrews provided, especially regarding her history of domestic abuse. Yet without his help in writing and presenting the letter, her claims were weak and not fully backed by legal evidence. Andrews did not visit her from the point of her sentencing and prepared for her trials without ever speaking to her. Furthermore, she could have claimed that his services were provided against American Bar Association rules, which prohibit the trade of legal services for copyright issues, such as the rights to her case. None of this was raised by her against him, and as such it was not considered during her habeas corpus appeal.

However on the 27th of June her appeal for state habeas corpus was turned away. She was placed in the position of proving that, had E. Ray Andrews presented a testimony about her lack of awareness of the insurance and her history of domestic violence, the jury would have judged her not guilty of a capital crime. Without a proper attorney to defend her, it would be impossible for Betty Lou to prove this was the case, and the court deemed Andrews's mistakes to have been harmless to her trial. The Fifth Circuit Court of Appeals went on to turn down her final appeals. The judges remained convinced that, regardless of any remaining evidence, Betty Lou Beets's history of violence and attempted murder, along with the two concealed bodies in her garden, were evidence enough that a death sentence was a fair response to the crime that had taken place. She had displayed violence her whole life, even towards men who had not presented a threat to her, and had attempted to kill all but one of her husbands. She had concealed her murders carefully and for many years and was willing to place the blame on her own adult son. In other words, regardless of her own situation, her criminal intent was viewed as evident and incorrigible, and her death sentence was the only fitting end to her crime spree.

On death row, Betty Lou Beets retained some supporters, mostly her own children. Some of Betty Lou's daughters went to E. Ray Andrews with photographic evidence of the domestic abuse she had suffered in order to request a parole review, but were declined. They insisted on presenting the evidence that she had suffered and that her acts of violence were a result of brain damage and abuse, not of malicious intent. Faye Lane, one of her daughters, insisted that her mother would only have done anything so horrific if she believed she was abused. Domestic violence awareness groups and charities acting against the death sentence appealed to have her sentence changed to a life sentence in prison, based not only on her own suffering, but on their universal stance against the irreversible process of the death penalty. Yet even those defending her maintained that she was a violent, unpredictable woman and not safe to exit into the general public.

And not all her children were so kind. Shirley told the press that Doyle Wayne Barker was killed because he owned the trailer where they lived, and that after the divorce which Barker had initiated, Betty Lou and her children would be evicted from the trailer and left homeless. This set a precedent where even her own daughter could not believe that Betty Lou was completely unaware of the financial benefits of murdering Jimmy Don Beets, especially not after she had successfully killed Barker. Knowing that she was still doubted and seeing hope as ever distant, Betty Lou composed her memoirs from death row, presenting her case.

Beets turned to her last resort which was to appeal to then-governor George W. Bush to spare her life. After a media incident where he jokingly insulted the last woman to be executed in Texas in an insensitive manner, George W. Bush seemed keen to prove he had no bias against women, even in the prison system, and agreed to review her case. This would have meant hearing the witnesses which had not been heard by the trial lawyer and present a case against her execution based on the circumstances of her life, including medical and psychiatric evidence. He could have granted her a thirty day reprieve in which he made his decision, however this never materialized. His number was made available and he received thousands of calls and letters from people urging him to spare her, with only fifty seven endorsing her sentence. Yet he did not grant the reprieve or halt the execution.

Betty Lou Beets was finally executed on the 24th of February of 2000, via lethal injection. Protestors from various organisations gathered outside as her sentence awaited. She declined both her last meal and her final statement, having been given by then enough time to make sense of what was happening and to say everything which needed to be said. Strapped to the death chamber gurney, she received her injection at six pm and died within eighteen minutes. She was sixty two years old. She left behind five adult children, nine grandchildren and six great-grandchildren, as well as her memoirs. Her story may be shocking, and it may be hard to pick sides at times, but that is exactly why her trial presents a solid case against the black and white ideals the court system held regarding crime and punishment, perpetrator and victim, defence and offence. Someone can at once be a victim of horrific crimes and a perpetrator of them, at once be a defendant and raise accusations, at once deserve punishment yet suffer a crime gone unpunished. There is no doubt that Betty Lou Beets was a violent woman who invited violence into her own life, an alcoholic and a murderer. However there is no doubt either that she was a good mother within her capacity, a victim of a series of horrific crimes, a disabled person with a background she could not escape and a desperate woman who saw no way out of her situation. Neither black nor white, good not bad, Betty Lou Beets sits in the grey areas of the law.

BLACK WIDOW JANIE LOU GIBBS

JANE CARLISLE

Janie Lou Hickox was born on December 25th, Christmas day, 1932 in Cordele, Georgia. Cordele is now a town with just over 11 000 residents, and is proudly known as the Watermelon Capital of the World. The city is named after Cordelia Hawkins who was the eldest daughter of Colonel Samuel Hawkins, the president of the Savannah, Americus and Montgomery Railway. In November of 1864, the area temporarily served as the capital of Georgia, but Cordele as it is now knows was founded in 1888 as a junction between two major railroads: the Savannah, Americus and Montgomery line and the Georgia Southern and Florida. Notable people from the area include jazz and blues singers, sportsmen, a White House Press Secretary and the president of an international Christian TV network. Nobody suspected that a serial killer who would be a black widow was growing up in their midst.

There is not much information about Janie's upbringing, but it was strictly religious and she grew up in a fairly poor family. Janie was married to Charles Clayton Gibbs, a farmer, when she was only fifteen. The two moved to the nearby town of Arabi which was just under ten miles away from Cordele, a mere fifteen minutes by car. Both of these towns fall under the Crisp County district. Arabi now has a population of 586, with 185 hosueholds and 125 families living in the town. Janie and Charles were regular churchgoers, and they had three boys: Roger Ludean Gibbs, Melvin Watess Gibbs, and Marvin Ronald Gibbs. For eighteen years, they lived quiet and devoted lives on the farm until tragedy began to take blow after blow upon the family.

Janie was known for spending all of her spare time helping out at the church and for her day-care service that she ran in her home for children of working mothers. Accounts note that on most days Janie would have around twenty-five children at her house aside from her own sons. While some believed her to have almost fanatic religious beliefs, all members of Janie's church and community believed her to be sound of mind and to know the difference between right and wrong, testimonies that they would later make in the investigation. Nobody felt that Janie had any emotional or mental issues, and simply knew her as a devoted mother who held God and the church close to her heart. When she wasn't looking after children in the community, Janie was helping out with events around the church and other ways to support the congregation.

Just before the tragedies began to occur, Janie had travelled to Albany, Georgia for a doctor's appointment. There she had been diagnosed with Lou Gehrig's disease, a motor neurone disease that destroys muscle control, is also known as amyotrophic lateral sclerosis or ALS. The disease progresses from a stiffness of muscles to twitching while the person becomes increasingly weaker. Eventually, once their muscles have decreased in size enough, the patient has trouble with speaking, swallowing, and eventually breathing. Janie was very aware that her body would begin to systematically shut itself down. After her trial, her defense lawyer Frank Martin stated that this was one of the most tragic aspects of the case as far as he was concerned. Frank believed that due to Janie's acute awareness of how her illness would progress paired with her fanatic religious beliefs, she wanted everybody that was close to her in the world to go to heaven so that she would be with them when she finally passed. Although Janie never admitted this in court, the murder of her husband, three sons, and grandson, all of whom she loved dearly, suggests that this might have been a contributing factor to the decisions or delirium that ended in her intentionally poisoning five members of her family.

The first member of the family to go was her husband, Charles Clayton Gibbs, who died on the 21st January 1966 when he was only thirty-nine years old. Janie was an avid cook, and she always had home cooked meals ready for her family when they returned home from work or school. After having had one such meal, Charles collapsed in the family home and was taken to hospital. Janie went to the hospital to care for him and brought a flask of soup with her. After Charles was served this final meal, he died painfully from stomach cramps and convulsions. Years later, investigators realized that this soup must have been laced with a particularly strong dose of arsenic from rat poison that Janie had been giving him in trace amount in his meals and coffees.

When administered in small amounts like this, it can be very difficult to determine if somebody is a victim of arsenic poisoning unless a doctor thinks to specifically check for it. Arsenic poisoning can result in a host of different symptoms and organ failures, so it is often the case that medical professionals are waiting for more evidence to be able to provide a solid diagnosis while the victim continues to be poisoned by somebody close to them. Symptoms can include abdominal pain and cramping, diarrhea, vomiting, dark urine, dehydration, vertigo, delirium, shock, hair loss, and convulsions. Arsenic is flavorless and odorless, making it very difficult for somebody to connect their normal food and beverage consumption with their illness. Arsenic poisoning can affect the skin, liver, lungs, and kidneys, which is both why it is such a potentially fatal condition and why it is difficult to detect without a hunch. In the case of Charles, his death was written down to an undiagnosed liver disease that he had been suffering for some time. While the doctors wanted to perform an autopsy on her husband to be sure, Janie said that she didn't want him 'all cut up', and her wishes were respected.

The church community provided an overwhelming amount of support for the Gibbs family once Charles had passed. The entire congregation was shocked, Charles having seemed to be in such good health until recent times, and also because he was still so young. The Gibbs family were provided with company, meals, emotional support, and everything that the members of their church community could possibly extend. When the life insurance claim for Charles came through, Janie donated a significant portion of these funds to the church to demonstrate her thanks for everything that they had done and her belief in the community. Janie claimed that she and the boys would have to continue on as best they could, and that she felt that with the strength of the church community behind them they would be able to make it through. Even after their home burned down soon after Charles' death and the family moved back to Janie's home town of Cordele, Janie continued to offer day-care services for the children of working mothers. There has never been an investigation into the house burning down, but the timing is certainly curious. Is it possible that Janie felt this was the only way to justify moving her family back to her home town of Cordele? It is clear from the rest of her actions over this two year period that she wasn't thinking rationally, and perhaps she wanted to escape the physical environment where she had been married for all of those years. Whatever the reason, just as nobody suspected that Janie had anything to do with the death of her husband, there was no investigation into whether or not the house burned down due to arson.

It was around this time that the oldest Gibbs son Roger took notice of a girl in their congregation, Ellen Penny. A relationship began to blossom between them under the watchful eye of Janie. The two teenagers began to spend more and more time together at church events, and participated in the same activities together. If Roger was assigned the duty of retrieving the bibles at the end of a ceremony, Ellen would always be there too help him. Very soon the two began to date. Over the next year Roger and Ellen married and she became pregnant with their first child. Ellen began living at the Gibb's residence, but this relationship and pregnancy was against a dark backdrop. It is difficult to say whether Janie took an immediate dislike to Ellen, or whether she did not want her son getting married and having a child so early like she had herself. Perhaps she wanted a different life for him, or harbored some resentment on being married off at such a young age. Either way, Janie never had a good relationship with Ellen and many times would behave as if she almost didn't register her existence.

Only months after Charles' death, Marvin began to develop the same symptoms as his father had. Having moved house and town, perhaps the rest of the family felt a separation with losing their father and like this wouldn't happen again with their youngest brother. There are no records of comments from the brothers or the community being concerned that Marvin would go the same way as his father, but sure enough, nine months after his father had died, Marvin Ronald Gibbs died on the 29th August 1966. Marvin too was determined to have an undiagnosed liver disease just like his father had, and Janie once again refused to have an autopsy performed. Perhaps Janie felt that performing an autopsy was an ungodly act that would in some way affect the chances of her family members getting into heaven? While the largest reason was most certainly to protect her own interests and for her to be able to complete her task, autopsy is a process rejected by many faiths and traditions. The police and staff at the insurance company pushed for autopsies as they felt that two deaths of this nature so close together and in one family didn't make sense. At this time, some members of the church community began to have suspicions about the deaths in the Gibbs family, but nobody wanted to be the one to come forward and accuse the pious and highly involved church member that Janie was. For many, there was still a huge disconnect. So even though the insurance company and the police of Crisp County were pressing for an autopsy on the body of young Marvin, Janie still had the support of the community enough to request that this procedure not be undertaken. Despite their suspicions, many in the community still felt that Janie wouldn't be capable of doing such a thing, particularly when it was to her own family that she seemed to have such an active devotion to.

Once again the church community poured support for the Gibb's family, offering counsel and companionship for Janie and her two remaining boys. When Marvin's life insurance came through, Janie once again provided a large portion of this claim to the church, which was undergoing significant renovations. While some began to talk about Janie seeming to almost be enjoying her new lifestyle, never being seen in the same dress and buying a new car, they could not help notice how generous she was also being with these funds. Those members of the community who still had faith in Janie chalked this spending down to a way to cope with her losses. However, Ellen Penny remained highly suspicious of Janie Gibbs. She didn't know how to speak out about her, both because she needed to live with the family and because she was so young, but after Marvin's death Ellen was certain that what was happening to the Gibbs family was no random or hereditary tragedy. Then, Melvin also began to fall ill.

As Melvin (often referred to in some articles as Lester) began to follow the path of his father and younger brother, the sixteen year old started to experience dizzy spells. Some people in the community attributed these headaches to puberty as the boy was sixteen. By this point, with such serious difficulties in the family, it is a wonder that Melvin's complaints weren't taken more seriously. He went downhill sharply. The doctors, not wanting to claim his death as another bout of undiagnosed liver disease that they weren't certain of, labeled his death a result of hepatitis. Once again a claim was made for life insurance, a portion donated to the church, and support lavished upon the Gibbs' family. At this point, Ellen became terrified for the life of her husband, herself, and their unborn child.

About a month after Melvin's death, Ellen and Roger's baby, Raymond, was born. Everybody noticed that Janie's mood lifted, and the community felt that this is where the horror ended for the Gibb's family. Janie was thrilled with her grandson, even though she had been so early married herself and her son had had his first child so early, making Janie a grandmother at thirty-four. Janie often used to show the baby to anybody who came around to the house, and would often be seen out with Raymond around the city. Ellen began to feel at ease around this time as Janie seemed to have changed entirely. The way that she interacted with Ellen seemed to have improved, and it seemed that the way that Janie went about all of her daily tasks with a different air.

However, even the baby began to fall ill soon. Ellen was in a state of desperation and didn't know what to do, the child only being one month old. The young girl has nobody that she could turn to, and didn't feel confident enough to make an accusation against Janie, even to her own husband. Despite the fact that Raymond was perfectly healthy, he died of an apparent heart condition. Everybody who was close to the Gibbs were completely shocked to hear of Raymond's death, and this is the point that many members of the congregation became highly suspicious of Janie. However, nobody did anything to prevent her from claiming the fifth and final member of her immediate family, her eldest and grieving son, with both Roger and Ellen still living with her at the time.

In the weeks after their baby died, Roger began to fall ill. Ellen, who was still under twenty at this age, had still not found the courage or the means to speak out against Janie. This may have been due to her living situation, or perhaps due to the sudden death of her son, but as Roger grew increasingly ill Ellen could do nothing but watch him deteriorate. She notes that during this time her husband constantly had red eyes, had visible rings around these, and was always pale and lacking in energy. He also used to get very severe headaches, but wasn't the type of person that liked to talk about any suffering that he was experiencing. The most that he would discuss these headaches was when he would be in such pain that he would be flinching. Ellen would ask if his head was giving him trouble again, to which he would respond with short and basic answers. Roger eventually found himself bedridden, being cared for by his mother. Despite what had happened to his father, two brothers, and own son, Roger never shared any suspicions about his mother with Ellen. It is entirely possible that he had figured out what was going on, being the last left, but didn't know how to get himself out of the situation.

Over the weeks, Roger's health got worse and worse. Ellen remembers overhearing an argument between Roger and his mother where he was repeatedly saying

"You did it! You did this to me!"

He was saying it over and over again as fiercely as he was able to in his deteriorated state. Ellen did not fully understand the conversation as she made sure that she kept out of sight. She asked Roger about it later in private, but he didn't reveal anything further and simply said that he and his mother had been squabbling over something. Ellen began to wonder whether she was paranoid about the situation, but it seemed that everything was pointing towards Janie's involvement in not only Roger's sickness but the suspicious deaths of the other four. Ellen stayed by her husband and cared for him as best she could, watching on as Janie nursed her son.

When Roger was eventually placed in hospital, Janie and Ellen spent nearly all of their time there. After a couple of days, Ellen noticed that Janie was in the habit of taking the water jug that the hospital placed in their room, tipping it down the sink, and replacing it with her own water. When Ellen asked her why she was doing this, Janie claimed that the hospital water had too much sulfur and that it hurt his throat. It was later realized that she was feeding her last remaining immediate family member increasing doses of arsenic through the water. Janie forced Roger to drink the water in large gulps and often. Once again, it is difficult to understand why this behavior was accepted by nurses, and also why nobody gave Roger testing for arsenic poisoning when four members of his family had died so suspiciously. However, even though this was a fairly common way for women to kill at the time, it is not until later years that we realized the signs and hints that might have saved the Gibbs family from their wife and mother.

One day, Janie asked Ellen to give Roger some water. Janie filled up a tall glass and placed it in Ellen's hand. Ellen gave Roger a small sip, but Janie demanded that he finish the whole glass, telling her that his throat is dry and he needs more. Ellen tipped the whole glass of water down her husband's throat, unknowingly giving him the final and strongest dose of arsenic. Perhaps Janie had been hoping that the blame might be placed on Ellen, or maybe she got satisfaction out of Ellen being the one that finally killed Roger, Janie having never been too keen on the girl. As Janie didn't want an autopsy on Roger, just like it was for the others, it is hard to say whether this act was a final insurance in her mind of her not being guilty of the crime, or whether it was the latter and she got satisfaction out of Ellen killing her spouse unintentionally. It is also possible, with Roger being left for last, that she was the least willing to kill him and needed Ellen to perform this final duty. After all, it would have made sense to kill the older two sons first and leave the younger one in her care, Marvin being so young and the least able of all three brothers to be able to take any action against his mother even if he had figured out what was happening. This suggests that Roger might have been somewhat of a favorite of Janie's, and that she wanted as much time with him as she could. Whatever the reason, Roger died soon after receiving the dose. He was only nineteen, and this finished Janie's work, whether it was insurance fraud or what she perceived to be God's work.

Just as she had with her two younger sons and her husband, Janie attempted to stop medical professionals from undertaking autopsies on Roger and Raymond Gibbs. However, as Ellen was the wife and mother, she has the rights of next of kin. Autopsies were performed that revealed extremely high levels of arsenic in Roger's organs, around twenty times that which you would expect to find in a body during an autopsy where arsenic has not been the cause of death. It was at this time that the Crisp County police called for the bodies of Charles, Marvin, and Melvin to be exhumed. People crowded around at the graveyard to watch while the bodies were taken out of the ground and placed on blue tarps. People began to say that they had thought there was something suspicious the whole time. A lot of guilt began to spread through the community. What if they had mentioned something earlier? Would they have at least been able to save the lives of Roger and his infant son? Mothers who had given their children to Janie to look after day in and day out felt embarrassed about their judgment of her character. This time the sympathy poured out for young Ellen who has lost her home, husband, and baby all within the space of a month. All five murders were committed in a short period of time, between 1966 and 1967. In all, Janie had received $31 000 in life insurance payments and given around ten percent of this to the church, but now she would have to answer for the crimes that she had done against those in the world that trusted her the most. Eric Hickey who has performed a study on female serial killers including Janie Lou Gibbs in 1991 claims that "These are the *quiet killers*, every bit as lethal as male serial murderers, but we are seldom aware of one in our midst because of their low visibility." Hickey also found that it takes an average of eight years to catch a female serial killer, nearly double what it takes on average to identify and arrest male serial killers.

Janie was arrested on Christmas Eve 1967, the day before her thirty-fifth birthday. She admitted to having killed all five of her immediate family members, but claimed that she didn't have a motive for doing so. While many people claim that she did this for the insurance money, there is still the chance that she genuinely committed the crimes in the name of her fanatic religious beliefs, wanting her family to be with her in heaven.

By February, Janie was determined to be insane and not fit for a trial but it was still agreed that she should not be able to live out her life in the community as she had been before. Janie took up residence at a state mental hospital where she served as a hospital cook, living there until 1976. At this time, multiple people had testified that they thought Janie was aware enough of her actions that she should have to deal with their legal ramifications. On May 9th 1976, Janie was convicted for her crimes and handed down five life sentences, one for each family member that she had poisoned. Janie's sister came to visit her in an attempt to understand the things that Janie has done, but found that she was largely nonresponsive and bewildered. The first question that her sister asked was *Why did you kill your family, Janie?* To which Janie responded she didn't know. Her sister attempted again, saying *Do you feel guilty?* Janice once again responded that she didn't know, seeming to be removed and numbed to the situation. Her sister made one final attempt to reach out to Janie and understand what had happened, asking *Can I do anything to help you?* For the third time, Janie responded that she didn't know. Her sister continued to visit her in jail in an attempt to understand more about Janie, what she had done, and what she was going through. But it seemed that no matter how much she tried, Janie was like a shell of what she had previously been.

She came up for parole seventeen times but was denied on each occasion. In April of 1999, due to her failing health as a result of Parkinson's disease, Janie was released into her sister's care. The last years of her life were spent in a wheel chair at a nursing home in Douglasville, Georgia, where she died on February 7th 2010. She now rests in the Sunrise Memorial Gardens at Lithia Springs in Douglas County, Georgia.